A PECULIAR FRIEND

My Memoirs at 30

Seun Rominiyi

authorHOUSE®

AuthorHouse™ UK
1663 Liberty Drive
Bloomington, IN 47403 USA
www.authorhouse.co.uk
Phone: 0800.197.4150

Published by AuthorHouse 07/22/2016

ISBN: 978-1-5246-6097-0 (sc)
ISBN: 978-1-5246-6096-3 (e)

Print information available on the last page.

CONTENTS

The thief does not come except to steal, and to kill, and to destroy. I have come that they may have life, and that they may have it more abundantly.

—Jesus Christ of Nazareth (John 10:10)

Introduction

> *You are my friends if you do whatever I command you. No longer do I call you servants, for a servant does not know what his master is doing; but I have called you friends, for all things that I heard from My Father I have made known to you. You did not choose me. But I chose you and appointed you that you should go and bear fruit, and that your fruit should remain, that whatever you ask the Father in My name He may give you. These things I command you, that you love one another.*
>
> —*John 15:14–17*

Everyone, including those who don't believe God exists, has a version of who they think God is to them or others in their lives. However, there is an old adage which says "Tis I alone who can truly tell, wherein my shoes it hurts the most." People can tell you who *they* think God is, what He should be to you, and how you should relate to him, but the reality is that you can't put God in a box. You can only truly discover God for yourself, on your own personal journey of discovery. So although there are amazing people in your life that will encourage and inspire you, guide and help you on your journey, and love and nurture you with their own unique experiences, the responsibility is still yours to seek God out for yourself. It is in your own genuine and earnest search for God that you discover so much more than you set out to in the first place.

For instance, when I say, “Oh, God is so merciful,” you might consider that an overused phrase – another Christian cliché – but to me, who has encountered God as merciful, it means a whole lot more than just those mere five words. God is inexhaustible, and there is no limit to the depth of His character or how far and wide you are able to stretch Him. As a result, He is able to reveal Himself to as many as come looking for Him in truth, revealing Himself to each person in a truly special way that is peculiar to that person's situations and circumstances because He Himself created those circumstances.

The Lord offers more than just hearsay; He offers an encounter with Himself that soon becomes your audacity to stand in life, an encounter that can cause you to enjoy restful sleep even through storms and stand firm in the face of the oft-harsh realities of life. You then also come to a realisation that some of the things you love – your quirks, your gifts, your interests, your challenges and strengths, and even your failures and weaknesses – all play a major role in you fulfilling your life's purpose. The idea is to find Him first, and then voila! You've found your purpose!

I have also found that when we make the most of our journey with Christ here on earth, we truly leave behind an indelible mark. This mark is one of honesty, transparency, and authenticity, both with oneself and with others. These are three of the major requirements to living this life of freedom we have been called to and enjoying it to the fullest.

If you are from my country of birth, Nigeria, you'll probably agree that *being open* doesn't necessarily come naturally to us as a people. We use our fears that we may be judged, alienated, or mistreated as excuses for not sharing the real truth about our challenges and experiences. I've also found, however, that in my journey God will almost every time have me share my *unique experiences* that are full of life's lessons so that the neighbour who is now experiencing a similar problem can take encouragement from my experiences. In many instances, alongside my dedication to loving others, my story of weakness turned strength has been a healing balm of Gilead for many, often even more effective than my fiery faith sermons. That is to say that our personal testimonies are worth a whole lot more, especially when we are witnesses first-hand.

We frequently share faith stories of others and heroes we look up to, but many times we ignore our overwhelming personal victories. Perhaps we fear appearing weak, afraid that others, who are hiding their own victory logs, will raise eyebrows as if to ask, "What kind of challenge is that?" Contrary to the belief that vulnerability is a sign of weakness, I have actually found it to be an emblem of strength in my life; to truly open oneself up to others, exceeding their expectations by reassuring them that you *have* been there and can identify with what they are going through, takes great strength. This is what I seek to do in this book, to share with you the defining moments of my journey so far – my sadness and grief, my joy and gladness, and my defeats and, most importantly, victories. I also feel the need to emphasise the fact that I never won a single battle I fought myself. I always had a friend who was right there with me, remaining still and cheering for me at all times in all seasons and still doing so on a daily basis.

Though I have not lived that many years and do not claim to knowing everything about life, I still remain confident that I should share my story because of the hurdles and mountains I have faced in my life up until this moment. I have lived an adventurous and challenging but truly rewarding life. No one, certainly not me, ever embraces pain or difficulty, especially not the agony of waiting in darkness each day, longing to see some sunlight, hoping and dreaming for that great future that has been promised. In hindsight I can truly say I am grateful for my struggles and heartaches, because without them I wouldn't be the resilient and faith-filled woman that I am today, and I wouldn't be enjoying this intimately close relationship I have fostered and am still fostering with the one who is truly important in our lives. I truly appreciate the poignant thoughts of Saint Paul and Saint Peter in these biblical scriptures:

> *My brethren, count it all joy when you fall into various trials, knowing that the testing of your faith produces patience. But let patience have its perfect work, that you may be perfect and complete, lacking nothing.*
>
> *—James 1:2–4*

> *But may the God of all grace, who called us to His eternal glory by Christ Jesus, after you have suffered a while, perfect, establish, strengthen, and settle you.*
>
> *—1 Peter 5:10*

> *Who comforts us in all our tribulation, that we may be able to comfort those who are in any trouble, with the comfort with which we ourselves are comforted by God.*
>
> *—2 Corinthians 1:4*

In the world today, God is often painted as a fiery, wrathful, and all-consuming deity who desires nothing more than to burn an entire generation in the unquenchable fire of an eternal hell. My reality, however, has been a stark difference. Even through my hardships and in the midst of my worst suffering, God has only ever shown Himself to me to be a wonderfully compassionate and loving father.

We talk about the love of God and think we understand it, but it is deeper than our minds can fathom. Let's face it, God's love and grace has no limit, and there is nothing anyone can do about it. Yes, it is necessary to remind people of the final eternal damnation for those who refuse to accept Christ, but we cannot diminish the reality of the cross and the potency of its power that is able to turn a peasant into a king. The cross is so powerful that one only needs to believe in it for a total transformation. God offers us something more than just heaven or hell; He offers us an invitation to dine in His courts, a place we are unworthy of, yet he invites us not as servants but as *friends.*

> *For there is hope for a tree, If it is cut down, that it will sprout again, and that its tender shoots will not cease. Though its root may grow old in the earth, and its stump may die in the ground, yet at the scent of water it will bud and bring forth branches like a plant.*
>
> —*Job 14:7–13*

In honour of the one who changed my life and is still changing it radically, the one who has given me something more valuable than any earthly possession, status, or accolade that one may desire in life, I give a part of myself to you. As I reach this milestone age, I offer my life as a testimony, in the hope that it changes your view of who God is and awakens the desire in you to pursue a healthy and honest relationship with your Creator.

I am reaching out to those who have hidden themselves away in emotional pits and those who have fallen and are left with only a blurry vision of their dreams, passions, and zest for life. I'm reaching out to the destitute and those left with nothing at all, on the verge of giving up on life, as I once was at a time in my life. It's easy to get swallowed up by the hardships and unnecessary burdens that life sometimes brings. Trying to live out a consecrated Christian life can be complex and difficult in our challenging world. We also suffer from the added pressure of aspiring to be a "somebody", expectations set by ordinary people as a yardstick for who can be considered distinct in life. These expectations are often set by worldly standards and more extreme perspectives.

A truth still remains: we only know in part, and so what people often think is the end may be just the beginning. There is no life that cannot be fixed, no matter how broken it may be on this side of kingdom life.

I am reaching out to those whose families or friends have given up on them and to those who are held bound by their insecurities, either from being bullied mentally by society, intimidated by societal pressures, or condemned by their own mistakes. There is hope for you in a sincere relationship with Christ. He can be a close friend to you, as he has been and still is to me.

I hope you find peace as you read this book, and I pray that you find the release to truly live out the life that you have been called to live, not free of challenges but free of defeats and perhaps not winning every battle but certainly winning every war.

> *The Spirit of the Lord God is upon Me, because the LORD has anointed Me To preach good tidings to the poor; He has sent Me to heal the broken hearted, to proclaim liberty to the captives, and the opening of the prison to those who are bound; to proclaim the acceptable year of the LORD, and the day of vengeance of our God; to comfort all who mourn, to console those who mourn in Zion, to give them beauty for ashes, the oil of joy for mourning, the garment of praise for the spirit of heaviness; that they may be called trees of righteousness, the planting of the LORD, that He may be glorified.*
>
> *—Isaiah 61:1–3*

Dear Lord,

I am grateful for every moment in life. I am on my way to doing that which I've always been passionate about. Thank You for the vision, goals, and so on that You've placed in my heart. Help me to be the best me that I can be. Help me to endure whatever is thrown at me, because in my weakness Your strength is made perfect.

May I not die with all my dreams and visions. Give me the strength to push forward against all odds.

You are the absolute best thing that has happened to me.

PS. I'm sat here at work feeling a little insecure. I know the gifts You've given me, but I can't help feeling a little left out when it seems like I keep messing up every now and again in my role.

Chapter 1

Growing Up

As Christians, we all have one story or another to tell about when we first began our faith journey in life, when we first began to accept the reality of a higher being in the heavens, a higher power than our fellow human beings. Most of our initial preconceptions or beliefs stem from our family life, upbringing, and culture. People who were initially not brought up in the way of the Lord often end up choosing paths filled with many twists and turns before they eventually meet their Maker. Thank God for His mercies, as He always causes all things to work together for our good. So no matter how far away one may have strayed and no matter how lost one may be, with or without God in one's life, there is no history God isn't able to rewrite. However, the importance of bringing children up in the way of the Lord can never be overemphasised.

> *Train up a child in the way he should go, and when he is old he will not depart from it.*
>
> *—Proverbs 22:6*

I must thank my parents for all their efforts in raising my siblings and me. Like all other parents, they were not without flaws, but they ensured we set off in life with the right guidance. They taught us that there was a higher authority to whom we owed our lives. I gained much from my father's love of espousing the biblical books of Proverbs and Ecclesiastes as well as my mum's insistence that we observe devotion every morning (where my siblings and I mostly farted and slept on our knees, only to echo a very loud amen in the end). I can even say that I appreciated the compulsory attendance at church, which also happened to be the only time I was allowed to put on my best clothes and shoes. As I'm sure you know if your parents were old school like mine, I also needed a hat to finish off the look.

My siblings and I never really understood why we did the things we did, but we obeyed our parents anyway; they were the vessels through which God gave us life. I never had a relationship with this amazing invisible person my parents seemed to adore so much, but for some weird reason, my parents did. Amusingly, they also seemed somewhat content with that situation as long as we complied with their rules and regulations whilst living under their roof.

We would sometimes read Bible passages, join Sunday school classes, and learn Sunday school songs, like this song sung to the tune of the French nursery rhyme "Frère Jacques": "I love Jesus; I love Jesus. He's my friend; He's my friend. He will never leave me; He will never leave me. He's my friend; He's my friend."

We also studied Bible stories that for the most part painted a picture of punishment for wrongdoing and left us with so many questions about God, the Bible, and Christianity that our Sunday school teachers often couldn't answer all of them. Bear in mind that, according to our culture, we were never allowed to question adults. Minors simply had to accept the belief that adults were always right. It was called respect, and till this day, I am glad I grew up knowing how to respect the elders in my life. However, growing up believing that I was not able to ask questions or challenge those older than I was did lead to some negative aspects in my life.

Dear Lord,

God, You are the absolute best. Though my heart and flesh may fail, Lord, You are the strength of my life, my waymaker, rainmaker, friend, companion, comforter, and soothing balm. You are father to the fatherless, the mighty deliverer, lover of my soul, giver of life, forgiver of sins, giver of mercy, beautifier of my life, and my shield of hope and glory. You lift up my head. You give me joy and peace. You are my faithful one. You are wonderful.

Thank You, Father!

He who spares his rod hates his son, but he who loves him disciplines him promptly.
—Proverbs 13:24

No one will ever say they enjoyed every bit of being disciplined for the wrongs they committed growing up. I may not have agreed that the punishment was appropriate for the offence in every circumstance, but when I look back, I can understand my parents' hearts. My parents did what they needed to do to ensure that my siblings and I turned out well in life. For this I am truly grateful.

Many of us grew up accepting punishments of all kinds from our parents as immediate responses to wrongdoings. The scariest part was that we were never sure what to expect each time. In my home, my dad was utterly unpredictable with his disciplinary approach. My siblings and I could end up writing long apology letters or transcribing many verses from the book of Ecclesiastes. It may sound pretty strange, but you have to admit that it was an interesting approach to child discipline. My dad would also give us long lectures filled with quotes from famous people when we messed up in some way. (I should add that these quotes have lived with me all my life.) My siblings and I called such a lecture "the talk", and being the unwilling recipient of one was a clear sign that you were in major trouble.

My mum, on the other hand, was oftentimes the mediator when it seemed like Dad was really mad. She afforded us the grace of a warning – "*Ma nà é o*" ("I will beat you") – before she eventually dished out the *ábára* (a yoruba word for a spank on any part of your body) with a sharp *pankērē* (a Yoruba word for long cane). These punishments had such an impact on me that before I even *considered* committing the same offence again, I would stop and think about the exact implications of my decision. My parents' discipline, although painful at the time, proved effective in my life. It laid the foundations of my core values and taught me to make good judgements after I grew up and left home.

At the same time, my parents were responsible, dependable, and accountable for school fees, summer lessons, and all the other bits and bobs a growing child needs. They were quite protective and never failed to show it when necessary.

I remember two major incidents quite vividly. After coming home from school with one earring in, my mum took me back to my primary school, where it emerged that the schoolteacher had stolen one of my earrings. Another time, my dad ended up taking a matter to the police station after a random security guard at our home was caught harassing me on the street (checking for God knows what on the body of a young girl at the tender age of 8). One thing was certain: my parents didn't mess about when it came to their kids. Today, I am still able to testify about this, and till this very day, when my father perceives I am struggling or having difficulties with anything, he always asks, "Shall I come down?"

Not only did my parents do their best to raise my siblings and me well, but they also accommodated and raised other kids as well. They extended the family, a philosophy I have certainly inherited. I grew up with distant relatives who soon became close family members. My parents looked after them as if they were their own, against all odds, even during later times when the adopted children became conflicted by thoughts that my parents were not their biological parents.

Another thing I will always admire is the fairness with which my parents raised us all. My parents treated my siblings and me the same and even taught us how to live with domestic staff without seeing ourselves as superior. (To be fair, this is something that is very common in Nigeria.) Whenever any of us attempted to disrespect the help, my parents were always quick to correct us. My parents taught us to see people first before social class.

My parents laid a strong foundation for us. They wanted the best for us, even though it sometimes seemed to us as if there was a conspiracy to cramp our style or make life miserable for us until our *real* parents suddenly emerged from where they had been hiding all this while to take us to our real homes.

Dear Lord,

Help me to evaluate my friendships. Sometimes I get hurt by pushing myself to be there for the people I love. Lord, I just want to obey You and surrender all I am to You. Flood my life with Your light; help me to be content in You. Help me to stop looking for love in the wrong places. Cleanse my heart.

Help me to be content with what You have given me so far in life. I have the best of everything, and there is more to come. I must believe this! I am so sad, but though we suffer in the body, our spirits move from glory to glory. I want a change in my life, Lord. I am so weak.

Please help me.

As much as my parents did to provide a safe, structured, and loving upbringing for my siblings and me (especially in terms of discipline), I admit that I would often just go through the motions of obeying my parents' rules. I never actually understood *why* my parents were telling me to do or not do something in the first place. This I can liken to the law that God gave the children of Israel in the Old Testament. Though the law was intended to instruct and guide the people of God on a path of success and prosperity, the people often struggled to fulfil it, for their desire was to disobedience and they had little understanding.

> *Do not think that I came to destroy the Law or the Prophets. I did not come to destroy but to fulfil.*
>
> *—Matthew 5:17*

> *But this is the covenant that I will make with the house of Israel after those days, says the Lord: I will put my law in their minds, and write it on their hearts; and I will be their God, and they shall be my people.*
>
> *—Jeremiah 31:33*

There comes a time in everyone's life where he or she needs to find God for himself or herself, finding that relationship that has been offered to us on a platter of gold by our Lord Christ Jesus. Almost everyone has a basic concept of morality informed by the Ten Commandments of the Old Testament scriptures, but we must move from this level of legality to a level of relationship with the Most High.

At the end of the day we don't really need to look that far to find Him. He is always there; we only need to awaken ourselves to the reality of there being a life in the Spirit. All parents, however great they are at parenting (which in itself is a praiseworthy achievement indeed), can only go so far in passing on certain ideals and values to their children. Only God truly owns every life, as parents are but custodians. And just as parents are on their own peculiar journeys, so are children. Whatever the case, it is important that parents bring up their children and guide them on the right path in life.

God is not a taskmaster. God is a loving father who is interested in every detail of our lives and who wants to see that we succeed.

Chapter 2

Finding Myself

That which is born of the flesh is flesh and that which is born of the Spirit is spirit. Do not marvel that I say to you, "You must be born again."

—John 3:6–7

No matter how close parents are to their children, even with a more modern style of parenting (in which children are encouraged to be open with their parents rather than simply being seen and not heard), every child has a side that he or she is unwilling to share with his or her parents, no matter how loving and supportive the parents are. Such a side remains solely under the remit of God. And so it is important that at a very young age, whilst the heart is still delicate and tender, children realise the need for repentance and spiritual rebirth. These early years are a critical time in young people's lives, representing a juncture where they begin to soul search for their Creator and make every effort to find Him through His Word and by the circumstances peculiar to their lives.

We all have a responsibility to accept Jesus as our personal Lord and Saviour. Our view and perspective of who God is oftentimes depends on the kind of home we were raised in and how we were raised. Some of us grew up in the church, having tagged along with Mum and Dad to every church meeting and special service. Some of us oftentimes had no choice in the matter, because our parents were pastors or ministers in the church. Some came upon the faith in their own lives, after growing up in a home that neither knew nor worshiped any god nor practised any religion for that matter. Whichever category one might fit into, one truth remains common: everyone needs to find himself or herself and, more importantly, needs to find God in order to continue on in life heading in the right direction.

In my own life, my revelation of God didn't come to me all at once, nor did God appear to me in a room with a triumphant entry and loud voice. But taking stock of my life now, I realise that each path I've walked on my journey has taught me a host of new things about who God is, His love for me, and His personal stake in my life. My parents were certainly instrumental in setting me off on this journey of discovering God.

> *Charge them that are rich in this world, that they be not highminded, nor trust in uncertain riches, but in the living God, who giveth us richly all things to enjoy; That they do good, that they be rich in good works, ready to distribute, willing to communicate; Laying up in store for themselves a good foundation against the time to come, that they may lay hold on eternal life.*
>
> *—1 Timothy 6:17–19 (KJV)*

One particular afternoon after school, I lay down fidgeting on my mum's bed, watching as she took out a large sum of money from her wardrobe. At the time I was content that things were finally working out for my parents. My dad had gotten a huge break in his business and was seeing the kind of success he been working hard for, for as long as I can remember. I leaned towards Mum, grinning from ear-to-ear at the money. Expressing my sheer excitement, I said, "We are rich, Mummy!"

I will never forget her response. She gave me this look, staring into my eyes. "We are not rich! We are OK. We are not suffering, but we are not rich," she scolded.

I remember being utterly confused. It wasn't until I was a lot older that I came to understand that her apprehension with my mindset was more to do with the wealth of my family getting into our heads. My mum didn't want us to become spoilt or ungrateful for how God had blessed our family. Me thinking we were rich would have been the beginning of that.

Dear Lord,

Feeling blah today. Things I would like to change about myself:

- *less talking*
- *more respect and caution with my husband*
- *self-control*
- *discipline*
- *closer relationship with God and a lot more forgiving of people*
- *more prudent in my spending*
- *more content and appreciative of what I have, whether friendships, clothes, money, or so on*

"Be content with obscurity, like Christ." Amen.

But godliness with contentment is great gain. For we brought nothing into this world, and it is certain we can carry nothing out. And having food and raiment let us be therewith content. But they that will be rich fall into temptation and a snare, and into many foolish and hurtful lusts, which drown men in destruction and perdition. For the love of money is the root of all evil: which while some coveted after, they have erred from the faith, and pierced themselves through with many sorrows.

—1 Timothy 6:6–10 (KJV)

Another thing I grew to appreciate about my parents was the fairness with which they raised my siblings, relatives and the domestic staff we grew up with. They treated my siblings and me the same in every respect and even taught us how to relate to the domestic help without feeling superior or haughty. Whenever any of us behaved in a way that could be seen as snooty or conceited, we would either be made to write an apology letter repeating the words "I will never do it again" over and over, to study the books of Proverbs and Ecclesiastes, or to be the unwilling recipient of a number of well-deserved lashes of the cane.

The following are just a few of my parents' favourite quotes:

Yet a little sleep, a little slumber, a little folding of the hands to sleep: So shall thy poverty come as one that travelleth; and thy want as an armed man.

—Proverbs 24:33–34 (KJV)

Omo ti o ba gba eko, a parun lojiji. (A child that rejects discipline will be easily destroyed.)

Pride goeth before destruction, and an haughty spirit before a fall.

—Proverbs 16:18 (KJV)

Children learn more from what you are than what you teach.

—W.E.B. Du Bois

> *Every man also to whom God hath given riches and wealth, and hath given him power to eat thereof, and to take his portion, and to rejoice in his labour; this is the gift of God.*
>
> *—Ecclesiastes 5:19 (KJV)*

> *Two things have I required of thee; deny me them not before I die: Remove far from me vanity and lies: give me neither poverty nor riches; feed me with food convenient for me: Lest I be full, and deny thee, and say, Who is the LORD? or lest I be poor, and steal, and take the name of my God in vain.*
>
> *—Proverbs 30:7–9 (KJV)*

> *I know both how to be abased, and I know how to abound: everywhere and in all things I am instructed both to be full and to be hungry, both to abound and to suffer need.*
>
> *—Philippians 4:12 (KJV)*

The absolute comfort zone is when you're in a place where there is no one else with whom to compare or measure your life. It's all nice and dandy to get all the attention drawn to yourself. After all, in the land of the blind, the one-eyed man is king. But then one day your parents pack your bag and whisk you off to a boarding school, one of the trendy ones at the time. Of course they want the very best for you, and so they advise that you also cut your hair so that you can focus and perhaps not have too much time for boys.

In such a situation, what do you do? How do you react or respond to this new environment? How do you accept the newly discovered harsh reality that "power surpasses power" (a cultural idiom meaning there's always someone richer, more powerful, or more successful than you)? You meet other kids who had very different upbringings from yours, and you realise that you're not all that special. You realise that amongst your new school peers there is wealth and there is *wealth.* Some kids, although paying the same tuition fees as you, enjoy the added benefits of summer vacations abroad, excessive pocket money, and the freedom to do as they please, whereas in your own case your parents take the time to painstakingly make every decision for you according to their own moral compasses. These other kids suddenly open your eyes to how plain you are as a person and to the many different reasons why you still don't fit in, despite the fact that your parents are also wealthy enough to pay those same tuition fees. How do you react to these intriguing new discoveries? Interesting, isn't it? I sincerely do sympathise with parents. Indeed, it was not easy for them, as much as it wasn't for me.

> *For we dare not make ourselves of the number, or compare ourselves with some that commend themselves: but they measuring themselves by themselves, and comparing themselves among themselves, are not wise.*
>
> *—2 Corinthians 10:12 (KJV)*

Secondary school for me was a very different ball game entirely. When I look back now, I see God's gracious hand upon my life, there were many instances like that, from deciding if it was OK to accept dance requests from boys at social nights (if they even asked me at all) to if it was OK to laugh along with students at teachers and many other teenage dramas.

Dear Lord,

Sometimes I feel funny about how I feel.

Help me to pull through with the things You've laid in my heart.

I love the song "You Covered Me" by Dr R.A. Vernon. Lord, help me to keep my thoughts only on You!

"You saw my needs when others saw my faults. You forgave me!"

Show me how real You are, dearest!

What I'd call my first instance of persecution for my beliefs occurred when I sternly warned one of my friends (talk about wearing my mother hen garment since the 1990s) to avoid a particular dance that we referred to back then as "the modern dance". Even I never truly understood why I felt it was wrong. Something inside of me just struggled to accept the butterfly dance, with its flexing, twisting, and rolling. My parents didn't teach those things to me, and as far as I was concerned, whatever we didn't do at home was wrong. A pretty interesting position for a teenager to have, right? Needless to say, after my attempt to rescue my dear friend from what I felt was her being wayward, I received terrible bashing from older students for being the party pooper. Their criticism was enough to keep me sulking for days.

I naturally swayed more towards playing the goody two shoes role, endeavouring to stay within familiar territory at all times. Looking back now, I find the whole thing pretty amusing. I realise now that there were many different types of students in my school: those with parents who wanted the best for their children and went to all lengths to find the money to provide it, those with averagely wealthy parents who had the means but were not prepared to give their kids anything they thought was unnecessary, and those with parents who had means and were ready to give their children anything they wanted regardless of its level of importance. The latter were the kids that I always felt envious of, but they were also the kind of kid my parents did everything they could to stop my siblings and me from becoming. They were the kids who got whatever they asked for from their parents. I would later learn that even God doesn't deal with us in this way, as His uttermost desire is to give us what is best for us as He deems fit.

In my secondary school, regardless of whatever category you fell into, you had to make a stand for something in order to survive. You could try to keep up with the Joneses, hide behind your mixed-race claim, study hard and get the honours of a bookworm, or be forced into friendships with those who couldn't care less about studying for themselves and who kept you around just in case they needed you in the exam hall. You could pretend you didn't care about anything and become the faux philosopher or, in some cases, genuinely become the voice of reason. You could even choose to play the sycophant in order to stay relevant. I wasn't quite sure where I fit in with all of this. However, at that time of my life, there was an expectation for people to be identified with something – either people or an ideal.

I longed to have all the stuff my peers had that made them shine. I desired summer vacations and Victoria's Secret matching lingerie. I wanted to strut around hostel corridors and be noticed for being really cute or just seeming international or continental. And in the social department? Forget it; I had no luck there either. I didn't get any Valentine's Day presents or awards for best this or best that. In short, I received no advances. I have no idea who or what contributed to the rumour that I wasn't to be messed around with. Perhaps my height and physique contributed to the reputation I somehow earned. Still, I enjoyed the reputation all the same; it was something to fall back on. After all, I would rather be respected for being strong and tough than be disrespected by little boys before the mocking eyes of my peers (I know beef). What was even funnier was that they all thought I was older than I really was, especially some of the boys. I did form quite healthy relationships in high school, but I was alone with my thoughts the majority of the time. On a few occasions when I became confrontational as a result of a conflict, I would find myself winning before the first physical tussle even took place. As they say, half the battle is usually won in the mind. Sigh. If only they had known my fears, my insecurities, my longings, and my desire to be relevant.

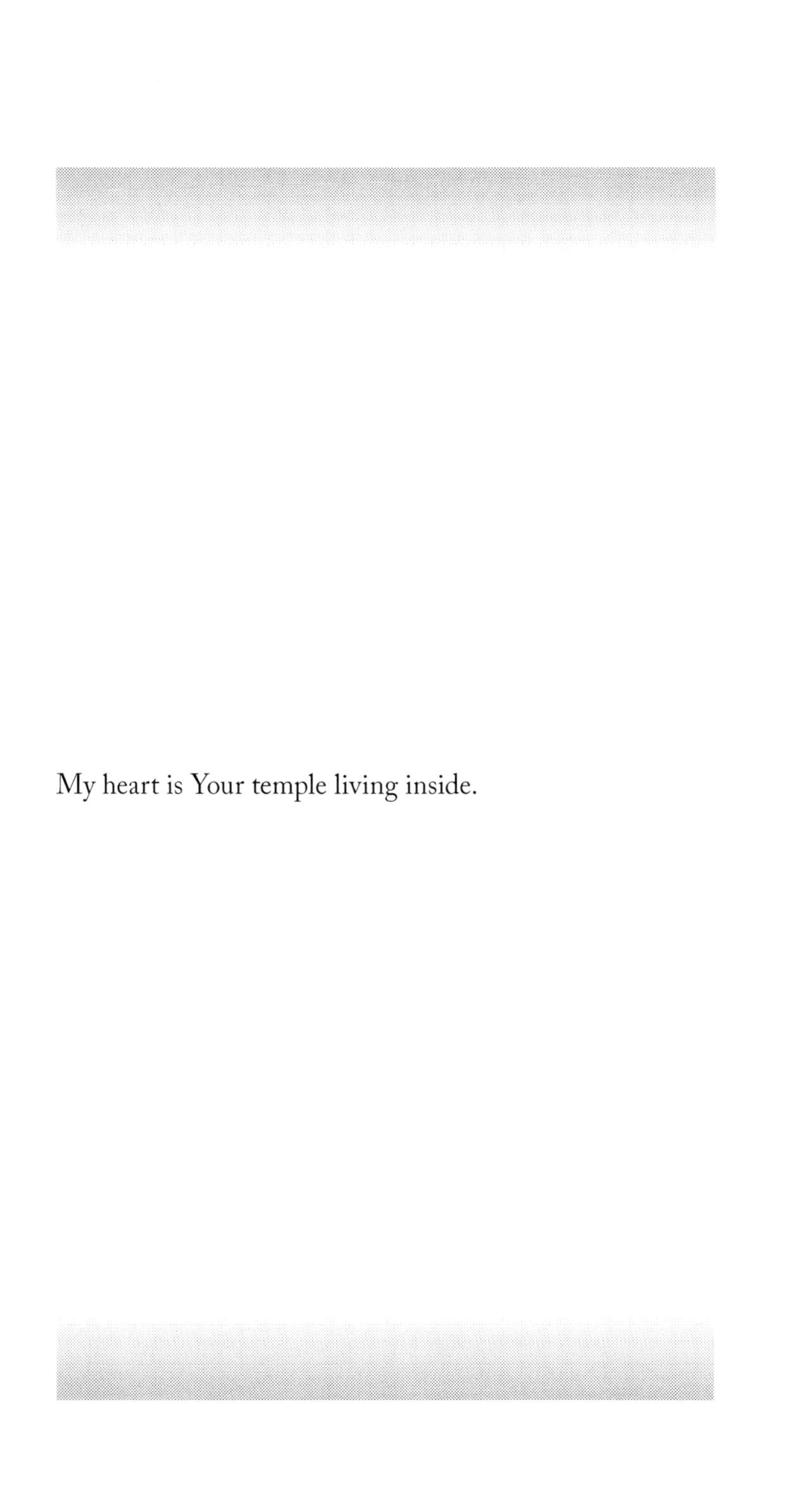

My heart is Your temple living inside.

All these factors contributed to my moody disposition when I was home on vacation. My parents suddenly had a silent contender in their home, but they never really realised it. I was always moody, frowning, and being overly sensitive – a lot of what we put under the banner of puberty these days. I had no one to honestly pour out my thoughts to, to talk to about how I felt and about my disappointment in the changes and battles of the mind I was now experiencing. No one had really warned me about the harsh realities of life and how I was to deal with them. So my coping mechanism was to put up a strong front, to make it seem that I was OK despite all my inner struggles. The technique worked as far as I was concerned at the time. It somehow managed to take me through high school until graduation, so it couldn't have been that bad.

The only boy I ever crushed on, I crushed on all throughout my high school years. He was a dear friend but was never really interested in me that way. It was not enough for me that I was oftentimes praised by my teachers for my positive attributes. It was not enough for me that I was seen as "good" sometimes. The idea of appearing good was weak in my then-myopic mind. Oftentimes whilst I was on vacation back home, I would enjoy the attention I received from the opposite sex on the street in the estate where we lived. I would get advances from thirsty-eyed men. Such advances were and I believe still are one of the challenges of any growing teenage child in my home country. Thank God my parents, especially my mum, were able to put strict controls in place. So although it was nice to get that sort of attention on holidays, it wasn't really the sort of attention that I was after. Attention from my circle, or my class, as people refer to it nowadays, was my ambition at that point, sadly.

> *Blessed is the man that endureth temptation: for when he is tried, he shall receive the crown of life, which the Lord hath promised to them that love him. Let no man say when he is tempted, I am tempted of God: for God cannot be tempted with evil, neither tempteth he any man: But every man is tempted, when he is drawn away of his own lust, and enticed. Then when lust hath conceived, it bringeth forth sin: and sin, when it is finished, bringeth forth death.*
>
> *—James 1:13–15 (KJV)*

The realities of desiring things like affection, relationships, and relevance became more awakened in me, and that right there was my cross. "Many of those who identify with my struggles likely shared similar crosses in their teenage years". It would form the beginning of my many insecurities. Maybe something was wrong with me, I often thought, because to be truly somebody, I thought I had to be accepted by everybody.

> *But lay up for yourselves treasures in heaven, where neither moth nor rust doth corrupt, and where thieves do not break through nor steal: For where your treasure is, there will your heart be also.*
>
> *—Matthew 6:20–21(KJV)*

It wasn't that being affluent was bad, but the struggles with wealth and the challenges associated with it were certainly demons I had to fight. Those from the Western world may not identify with these struggles, but certainly the people from my birth country can relate to it, given that more than half of the population of Nigeria lives in abject poverty, with so much cultural value placed on wealth and social status.

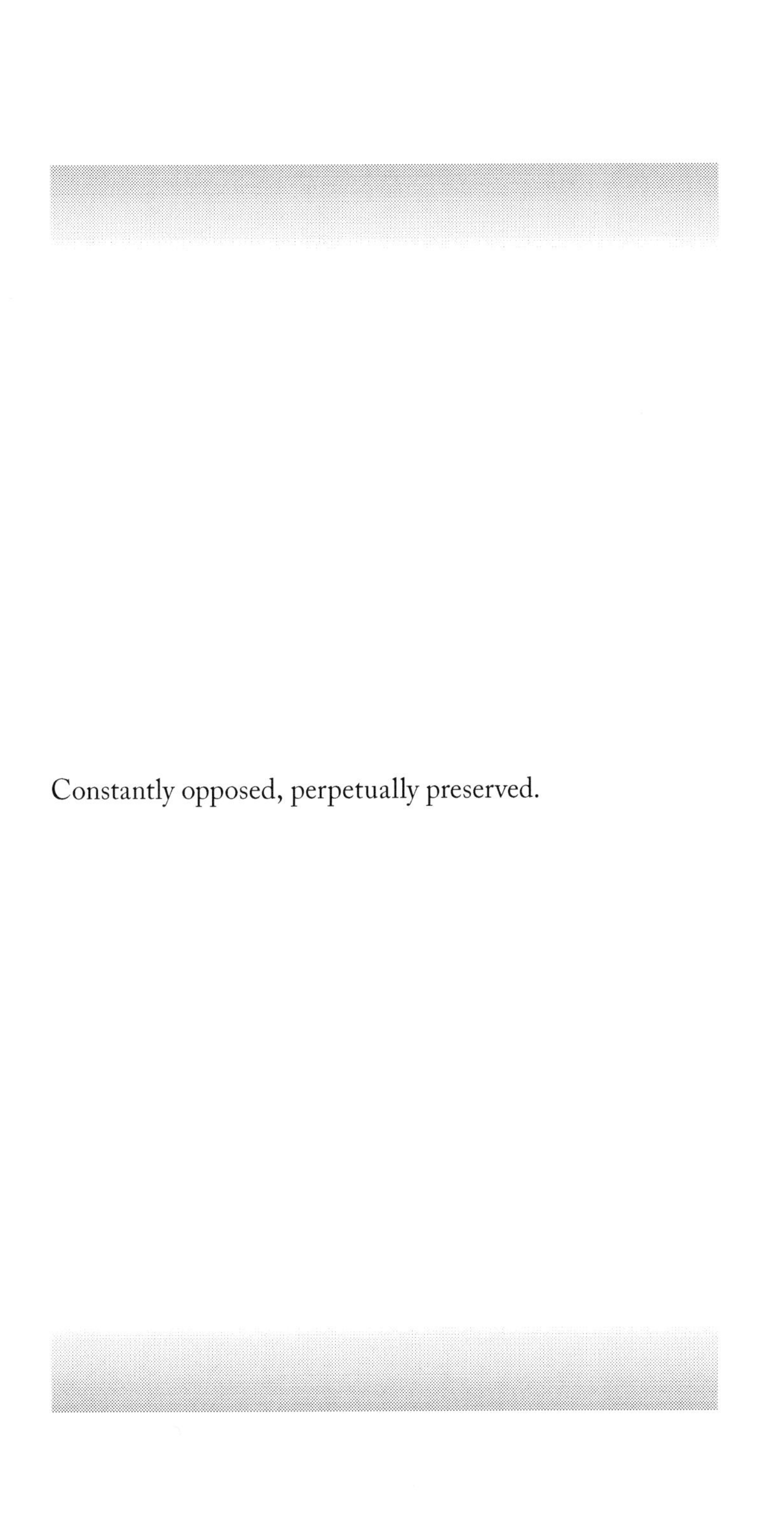

Constantly opposed, perpetually preserved.

In my world back then, money could speak and could serve as a weapon to intimidate, gain respect, and stay relevant. Some parents couldn't even correct their kids when the kids acted out of line with their domestic staff; after all, the parents treated the staff badly themselves. Sure there will always be the poor among us, but this warrants no superiority complex. These kids then brought that poisonous culture and mindset into school and used it to intimidate others. Some maybe didn't do so intentionally, but it certainly was the intention of the majority.

There was always something in my childhood that either made me leap for joy, like when my dad's driver picked me up in the latest Jeep my father had just recently acquired, or wallow in sadness, like when my mum received disapproving stares for riding on public transport for whatever reason. In my school I found that we the students sized others up in that same light. We very much held the general mindset that things were going well if one was fruitful externally, even if most of the time, if not all the time, one was perishing internally.

> *There is one who makes himself rich, yet has nothing; and one who makes himself poor, yet has great riches.*
>
> *—Proverbs 13:7*

> *And He said to them, "Take heed and beware of covetousness, for one's life does not consist in the abundance of the things he possesses."*
>
> *—Luke 12:15*

Another interesting dimension to this was that although these kids were getting all the attention one might desire, being in the limelight and appearing to have an added advantage over others, they never really had true friends. They horribly mocked and bullied others, physically or emotionally. There was always a darkness and gloominess that surrounded them. It was almost as if they had been enslaved to living up to the many expectations of others, both peers and teachers alike. Some of them were not even happy about the decisions they made or the lengths they went to in order to stay relevant. And guess who they would come to when they were bruised, looking for comfort in their grief – My friends and I. It's always been the trend even till now. Supposedly wealthy folks can find it really difficult to develop and keep authentic relationships in their lives.

> *There is a way that seems right to a man, but*
> *its end is the way of death.*
>
> *—Proverbs 14:12*

One sunny afternoon one of the popular girls at school called a meeting on our corridor. My goody two shoes friends and I decided to attend after hearing it was a very important meeting. It turned out its purpose was just for the girls to complain about some of the popular boys, who were allegedly being disrespectful. The girls said it was now time to put them in their place. The whole thing was initially quite amusing, until we realised that the girls were not joking. They talked about how the boys had started slapping girls and doing all those juvenile things associated with just being boys. We all nodded in agreement, but afterwards I went off with my friends making jokes about the whole thing. My friends and I didn't get involved. The next day the school block was silent, even the boys the girls had been complaining about, and the other boys knew there was some weird thing going on that day. It wasn't long before

I realised that it was such a stupid idea to fight battles that were not my own. After all, I had nothing to gain anyway. That day and many others like it, I exercised my freedom and enjoyed a mini victory.

My body might be dying, but I'll always be alive. Hope beyond the suffering, joy beyond the tears, peace in every tragedy.

> *Now we exhort you, brethren, warn those who are unruly, comfort the fainthearted, uphold the weak, be patient with all.*
>
> *—1 Thessalonians 5:14*

I oftentimes found the boldness and courage to stand up for myself and others even when I was trembling on the inside. For example, one time my friends and I were playfully singing along with the school drummer boys as we marched out of the assembly hall. All we were doing was singing along to a silly rhyme: "Your mumsi na monkey. Your popsi na handsome gorilla. No wonder you resemble handsome gorilla. No wonder all your people handsome chimpanzee." One of the popular girls screamed at us to shut up. I am not sure what it was that annoyed her; maybe she didn't like the fact that everyone else found it funny, or maybe she just wanted to exercise the strength of being one of the popular girls. After she shouted at us, a few people laughed it off, but I carried on. Call it being rebellious, but that day I wanted to prove a point at all costs. She might be one of the popular girls, but it meant absolutely nothing to me (or maybe it did mean something to me after all, who knows). Even though cold shivers were running down my back, I couldn't bear to satisfy the already wandering rumours that my friends and I all kissed bum, especially not in front of the popular boys. I wonder if I inherited this behaviour from one of my parents. (Shh! Don't tell them I said that!) In any case, in moments like that I knew I had strength, but then again, was it really mine?

> *The bows of the mighty men are broken, and those who stumbled are girded with strength.*
>
> *—1 Samuel 2:4*

> *Woe to those who go down to Egypt for help, and rely on horses, who trust in chariots because they are many, and in horsemen because they are very strong, but who do not look to the Holy One of Israel, nor seek the Lord!*
>
> —*Isaiah 31:1*

An interesting rush of emotions soon ensued after that episode. Although it felt good to appear as though I was winning, I also felt guilt and remorse, almost as if I owed the other person something. It was this remorse that stuck with me long after the incident.

Such guilt became more apparent in another incident, when I stood up for a dear friend of mine who I felt was being bullied emotionally by a girl whose strength wasn't necessarily in riches but more in her running mouth. I couldn't bear to watch the injustice and listen to the mocking voices from across the room. I eventually just lost it, and before you could say *owanbe*, I was in a verbal exchange myself with the bully.

As you might guess, one thing led to another, and the altercation ended up turning physical, only I was the only one throwing punches. I expected my blows to end my opponent's running mouth, but I was bitterly disappointed. The more I hit her, the more she retorted with a continuous barrage of verbal insults. I regretted my actions that day most certainly. I hated that I had been pushed that far, and I also didn't enjoy the attention from the onlookers who gathered around to watch the events unfold. The incident might have solidified my reputation of being a no-nonsense person or made me appear somewhat tough in the eyes of my peers, but it still didn't feel right.

I had been reprimanded by my parents up until that point in my life. I had been shown why I had to be sorry for the many misdeeds of my youth, like when I lied to my parents that a student in my primary class had cut my hair even though I was the culprit or the times when I sneaked back to watch TV past bedtime, earning me a spanking. Nothing had quite prepared me for the emotional turmoil I would suffer when there were no more immediate punishments and I was left alone with my conscience.

My parents did well in teaching me to say "thank you" and "I am sorry", but no one ever really taught me how to reduce the number of times I would have to make those apologies. Of course I was brave enough to walk up to the girl later on that day to express how sorry I was for what I'd done. There was something very profound to me about how emotional and genuinely sorry I was.

It's the darkest just before the dawn. Might be the hardest season. I know it hurts. Won't be too long. Help is on the way … You are closer than you think you are.

Look to the sky; help is on the way. Our God is faithful to say, "It's not over. It's not finished. It's not ending." It's only the beginning when God is in it. When God is in it, there is no limit.

Chapter 3

The Invisible Battles

For we do now wrestle against flesh and blood, but against principalities, against powers, against the rulers of the darkness of this age, against spiritual hosts of wickedness in the heavenly places.

—Ephesians 6:12

The challenges we face in life are shapeless puzzle pieces that will eventually come together in the future. Our struggles don't always make sense at the time, their purpose unclear until much later. When someone is suffering, how do you say with a strong conviction that everything will all work out and that it's going to be OK? How do you convince that person that this pain, terrible incident, or trial – perhaps horrible name-calling – is all working out for his or her good? With every new level, promotion, or graduation comes challenges and tests.

When I went to college after high school, I felt the usual apprehension of meeting new people and warming up to them. At this time in my life, at 17 years old, the task felt even more daunting. My self-consciousness was raised to the power of 100, and my insecurities were much more glaring. No one is born confident; most people can be insecure. The amount of insecurity differs from person to person based on each person's background and exposure to various situations. Some learn to manage their insecurities better than others and are able to recover a lot quicker.

Most people at the age of 17 are unlikely to understand the concept of not wrestling against flesh and blood, unless they are very familiar with the life-giving Word of God. What does that idea really mean to a 17-year-old, especially one not from a religious background? Not too many people understand that the weapons against faith are not necessarily obvious spiritual missiles like in Nollywood movies. Such weapons can be the carnal minds of other human beings like yourself who ignorantly allow themselves, knowingly or unknowingly, to be used by the Devil and his deceptive ways. Some of us get bound by such wounds and limitations for many years, being shaped and controlled by the consequences of those afflictions and never really understanding that the war is not with those humans but the Arch-enemy, the Devil. Thankfully Christ came to redeem us and set us free from such limitations. What most of us often miss is that the Enemy will always take advantage and prey on our weak spots and vulnerabilities. Nothing has ever changed about this approach since the world began.

> *But no man can tame the tongue. It is unruly evil, full of deadly poison.*
>
> —*James 3:8*

> *There is one who speaks like the piercings of a sword, But the tongue of the wise promotes health.*
>
> —*Proverbs 12:18*

So one day I was sitting peacefully in my room in the boarding facility my college institution provided. One of the new friends I had just made came in to share some information with me that she thought was important. I can understand her intention; she was only trying to be sweet. Little did she know, though, that this information would have a negative impact on my life. Her words went into my mind like a sinking ship. "You know those girls," she said, referring to the popular girls, "they said you are very ugly." I can't remember if I cried. I wasn't sure which was worse, what the girls had said or the sympathy my friend had for me. When I look back now, the whole thing seems a bit silly, but at the time it felt as if someone had stripped me naked and left me in the market square for everyone to watch. What I should have thrown in the bin became a false foundation for all my decisions. I clung to those lies as if my life depended on them. At the time I thought the people who said those things were the people who mattered the most, and so I thought their words had to be true. It was another opportunity to use the bin, but I found no strength to do so.

Every way of a man is right in his own eyes,
but the LORD weighs the hearts.

—Proverbs 21:2

> *He was a murderer from the beginning, and does not stand in the truth, because there is no truth in him. When he speaks a lie, he speaks from his own resources, for he is a liar and the father of it.*
>
> *—John 8:44*

> *Bless those who curse you, and pray for those who spitefully use you.*
>
> *—Luke 6:28*

I didn't have to confront these girls; I wasn't one to be confrontational. In fact, I continued in my hellos and my usual smiles, with the pain still in my side. I didn't have to fight back physically or even verbally; I was going to fight back by changing this view they had. I became even more conscious of myself, relating every negative thing that happened in my life from then on to the girls' hurtful words: "You are very ugly." Isn't this how we allow the Devil who can smell our fears and insecurities from afar, to whip us hard with painful words from people? This incident certainly didn't work out well for me, as I began to make external factors the reality and measurement for my success.

I carried this baggage around with me. I went about my day-to-day with insecurities around my neck. I still ensured commitment to my Sunday and midweek services but more as rituals than anything else. The sermons would pierce through and prick a bit but would never really pierce down into the marrows. As far as I was concerned, I was now a free bird with the liberty to do anything I desired. It felt good to be noticed eventually and felt great to be recognised for one thing related to social activities or the crème de la crème of my university days. i.e. getting involved in one way or the other.

With no parents to cramp my style, tell me what to do, or restrict my movements at the university, it was time to create the image I had always wanted for myself. Such false security led me into many downfalls and too many heartaches. In fact, this task of belonging was too great, greater than the simple task my parents gave me of bringing back home accounting and law degree certificates. This liberty, however, was the very platform by which I would learn life lessons even as I began my career journey. This was real life, like a friend usually says. It was real life indeed.

> *The LORD has appeared of old to me, saying: "Yes, I have loved you with an everlasting love; therefore, with loving kindness I have drawn you."*
>
> —*Jeremiah 31:3*

As a child, you never fully understand pain or challenges. You feel those heart palpitations or unsettling feelings that immediately prompt you to cry, drawing the attention of caring parents, relatives, or friends to come to your rescue. But as you grow older, a lot of the time the tears are iced up in your chest and difficult to express. The reality that bad things happen or the realisation of consequences hits you. Only then do you truly become aware of the harsh realities of challenges and stumbling blocks. Apart from the emotional challenges associated with relationships (which I will share in subsequent chapters), oftentimes things don't go the way we plan, either due to our own wrong choices or because life just happens. In some situations the more you try to bail yourself out, the messier it gets. There is, however, one common trend as we all go through our challenges or hurts: we are always looking for a saviour.

Always there, always available to catch even the shooting thoughts. Always there to catch the roaring thoughts of a troubled inner heart.

It is good for me that I have been afflicted, that I may learn your statutes.

—Psalm 119:71

Pains, challenges, and heartaches are reminders of our need for a superior power. It's only at these peculiar times that most of us come to know Christ, because when things are rosy and going well, we don't really need anybody. It's in the midst of our trials that we can truly see Jesus, how He turns things around and truly causes all things to work together for our good. We also need Him because He created us, and if there is indeed an Arch-enemy, you are better off on the side of the Creator.

Embracing the liberty of not having parents at the university and not being accountable to them, I didn't quite put in my best in my studies. I didn't do anything out of this world, staying within the confines of my home values with maybe a few deviations here and there, but I lived carelessly and didn't make the most of the opportunities or do the very best I was capable of doing. In my third year, when it finally dawned on me that my father was still expecting a huge investment on his returns (i.e., the popular first-class honours that Mr & Mrs Do No Bad in Our Eyes' kids had already gotten that had gotten them jobs at World Bank), I tried all I could do to redeem myself. I hoped that even if I couldn't make first-class honours, I could at least make second-class upper (which was second to best).

My first defeat was that I didn't dream of first-class honours; my second defeat was that I didn't work hard enough for my goals. I was preoccupied with frivolities and extracurricular activities that added no positive value to my life. I gave everything in that last year to redeem myself with my final project (dissertation).

One of my tutors assured me that I had already stepped into the second-class upper rank. I was so excited that I went round to broadcast the news. I shared the news with my family, friends, and anyone that cared to listen. They were proud of me, happy, and excited that I'd done really well. It was the best moment in my life. I could confidently share my rank because it was generally accepted as accurate by anyone who understood anything related to the higher institution.

Then the results were made public and put up on the wall in the second floor in my faculty block. With a spring in my step, I made my way with several other colleagues to see the results. As far as I was concerned, I was only going to confirm what I already knew. On getting to the list (thankfully we were identified by our designated numbers so others wouldn't know your grade, unless you had that one friend who knew your identification number), I discovered I'd earned second-class lower. I glanced through the list over and over again to be sure I had not picked the wrong identification number. The grade wouldn't disappear. It just sat there, refusing to be moved or swapped. It was the reality of my time at the university. I panicked and thought about all the people I had told about getting a 2:1 and about my dad and all the people he had shared this great news with. The shivers down my spine were the worst feeling ever. What was I going to do now? You know the saddest truth about all of this? I was more worried about what people would think than about the fact this rank showed one thing and one thing only: a reflection of my time at the university.

A better outlook would have been to forge ahead with the conviction that although a lecturer had seemed to decide my destiny by a grade on paper, there was one who was majorly responsible for deciding my destiny in reality.

You take our failures and our weakness, creating success and bringing strength from them. Out of ruins, You bring forth glorious treasures, making us into something even better.

For I know the thoughts that I think toward you, says the LORD, thoughts of peace and not of evil, to give you a future and a hope.
—Jeremiah 29:11

Now some people know how to party hard and faff around whilst working hard at the same time, but I've never been able to do that. I throw myself into things, and I can't throw myself into several things at the same time without one of them suffering.

I decided to meet with the tutor who had initially told me about my grade, and I learned I was only a mark away from this grade I now desperately desired. I tried everything to get the grade raised, but all my requests fell on deaf ears. The final letter I received on the matter made me weep for days. I was very heartbroken and inconsolable, despite numerous attempts from my best friend (hi, Dara Osinubi) and other friends. They told me that God was in the business of making the best out of bad situations and that there could possibly be a reason for how things had gone even though I was partly to blame and so on.

Now many people go through worse situations that cause them to mourn greatly. This is probably small in comparison to the terrible first challenges some people face in their early years. In my case, I perceived the grade as an attack on my reputation, the very thing I had now started preserving. My reputation was my security, so of course it made sense for the Enemy to attack me right there. How was I now going to go back and tell the many people I had told about my grade that actually it wasn't quite the truth? Those thoughts haunted me for days.

There is no fear in love; but perfect love casts out fear, because fear involves torment. But he who fears has not been made perfect in love.
—1 John 4:18

My thoughts consumed me each day. I kept telling my dad that the school was still trying to make a decision on my final grades. What he didn't know was that I had received a letter from the university encouraging me to move on from the defeat. In summary, the letter said that people often come into the higher institution with lots of expectations only for some to have their expectations unmet but that my perceived defeat didn't have to be the end of the road for me but an opportunity to take life by the horns and do better. Those words made absolutely no difference to me and meant absolutely nothing to me. If anything they made me weep even more.

I was filled with apprehension and discomfort at the thought of disappointing my dad, who believed so much in me and was expecting so much from me. All I could think about was my disturbing trip back from Benin City after a semester at high school when I hadn't done well. I recalled his stern look and concentration on my high school report card with Mummy by his side, all of us in absolute silence, waiting for the judge to deliver the verdict. It usually wasn't about what my dad said; it was mostly about what he didn't say. The more words, the better it was looking for me, but just a few words left me even more insecure. The difference now was that my dad wasn't able to check every semester. Perhaps he would have rung the alarm bells early, saving me from this annoying grade. Whenever he called to ask about school, I would say, "Everything is fine," and that was enough for him. I had grown up a little more, and my report assessments were no longer as frequent. This relates to our walk with God as well. His laws are written in our hearts. Repercussions may not be instant, but there are defining moments after a long haul in which we face consequences.

I prayed – oh, how I prayed – and remembered that there was indeed one who saved. My favourite four words are "Lord, please help me", and I would mutter this prayer under my breath every now and again. My dad knew there was something wrong and started asking questions, but all I said was a reassuring "I am fine." He knew what was upsetting me had to do with the result but wasn't quite sure why I was still carrying the trouble inside my head after several attempts of his to persuade me it was all going to be fine.

Then one morning he barged into my room and saw me on my knees saying my prayers. He left but then came back to ask that I come speak to him afterwards. When I went to speak to him, he asked, "What is bothering you, Seun? Is it your result?" I couldn't hold it in any longer. My heart melted, and I wept. I wept because straight away he knew what it was; he knew what was on my mind. I felt very naked because all along I had thought the burden was meant for me to carry all by myself. As soothing words of encouragement left my dad's mouth and dived into my heart, I couldn't believe his reaction this time around. He shared about his own failures in life and how he was now this great man today. *Indeed, we are encouraged by the strength of others but only really connect with their vulnerabilities.* I expected punishment but received love in abundance on that day. I received much more than I was anticipating. My dad showed me a glimpse of the grace and mercy I now enjoy from knowing Christ daily. Daddy was kind and merciful to me on that day. Oh, the freedom that overwhelmed my heart when the truth was out. The truth truly sets you free.

To achieve anything tangible in this life, you must learn to manage both internal and external reactions. Just keep your eyes on the ball; stay focused.

Chapter 4

Finding Jesus

I'd finished my undergraduate degrees. As I was not too impressed with my grades, I had developed a complex about finding a job. A friend of mine introduced me to a small company where she had done a work placement whilst studying at university. She was one of those one-step-ahead friends who seem to have it all together. I was really happy. This company didn't judge me by my grades but by recommendation, and that was quite encouraging. I interviewed and got the job. The handover and training was done in quite a hurry. In usual fashion I nodded my head in affirmation even when I didn't understand a thing. As it was a small company, there was no time for spoon-feeding anyone. As far as they were concerned, I interviewed and got my friend's old job.

> *For as he thinks in his heart, so is he. "Eat and drink!" he says to you, but his heart is not with you.*
>
> *—Proverbs 23:7*

Every single day on the job was painful. I couldn't sleep, because I was either worried sick about what catastrophe

I had committed that day or frightened by the thought of seeing both my bosses' faces the next day. Eventually they bade me farewell. I overheard my boss talking to someone on the phone about a new employee who was posting things wrongly and causing difficulties. I was then called to a corner and told that they now needed someone full-time, as they could no longer cope with part-time. Ouch! That didn't go down well at all. I felt as if I hadn't been trained enough and as if I wasn't good enough. I felt all kinds of ways when I could have simply owned up to not knowing much at the beginning. More sadly, I didn't believe in myself to start with. These and many other reasons birthed the idea of moving to London to study for my professional exams.

> *Your ears shall hear a word behind you, saying, "This is the way, walk in it," Whenever you turn to the right hand or whenever you turn to the left.*
>
> *—Isaiah 30:21*

My student visa was set to expire soon, and a conversation with my dad spurned me into action. "What is your plan? Do you want to move back to Nigeria or what?" my dad asked. Don't get me wrong; I love my home country, but I wasn't quite ready for that move just yet. I was so stressed out that I sold the idea to him of extending my visa by going back to school for a master's degree. My dearest dad, as always, bought into the idea, and with dearest mum in agreement, they provided me everything I needed for my studies. My dad recommended I go back to Luton, as it would be easier to get a spot at the university, seeing as I was already an alumnus. I didn't really want to go back. My memories of Luton weren't so great. I eventually gave in but decided to live in London and commute to Luton for my studies. As I walked home on the day I was told I had been offered admission, I heard these words in my heart: “Stay one more year. I have a plan for you.” I wasn’t sure if the words were just in my head, but I certainly felt peace about the decision I had made.

The wrong messages will make you passionate for the wrong things. They make you self-centred and unlike Christ.

Be careful what people say, and pay more attention to what God thinks.

—Pastor Mazino Egbuwoku

> *Moreover you shall say to them, "Thus says the Lord: 'Will they fall and not rise? Will one turn away and not return?'"*
>
> —*Jeremiah 8:4*

I have to admit that I had a blast in my master's degree programme. It was different from my previous schooling experiences, and I made a few good friends too. I became a little more confident in class and engaged with the process. Although I had to juggle my studies with the few other professional exams that were left of the ACCA, I finally felt as if I was heading towards achieving something great with my life. The Lord crowned my effort with a commendation alongside three others on graduation day. At the very place where I had been denied the joy of success, I was honoured with a commendation. It was so redeeming and vindicating, so fulfilling and refreshing. My proud father in his white regalia agbada grinned from ear-to-ear, enjoying the attention he received from those who were intrigued by his costume. This day truly made me see myself a little differently.

> *And I will pray the Father, and He will give you another Helper, that He may abide with you forever.*
>
> —*John 14:16*

I remember bumping into an old family friend from back home one fine sunny afternoon in the summer of 2008. It's amazing how God orchestrates some paths and guides us into His purpose for our lives. This friend soon introduced me to the Trinity Chapel. Trinity Chapel as I knew it then was a very vibrant church, not to say that it isn't now. It was very different from what I was used to and what I understood church to be. It was filled with young people like myself, on fire for God. If you judged them by their appearances, you would think, *What an unserious bunch.* The activities, the fun, the commitment – I had never seen anything like it. I looked forward to every waking Sunday. Maybe it was selecting an outfit or the journey or maybe even the new friendships I was now making; I don't know. It all seemed exciting at the time, and I kept going back over and over again, until one day the Lord meant business for me.

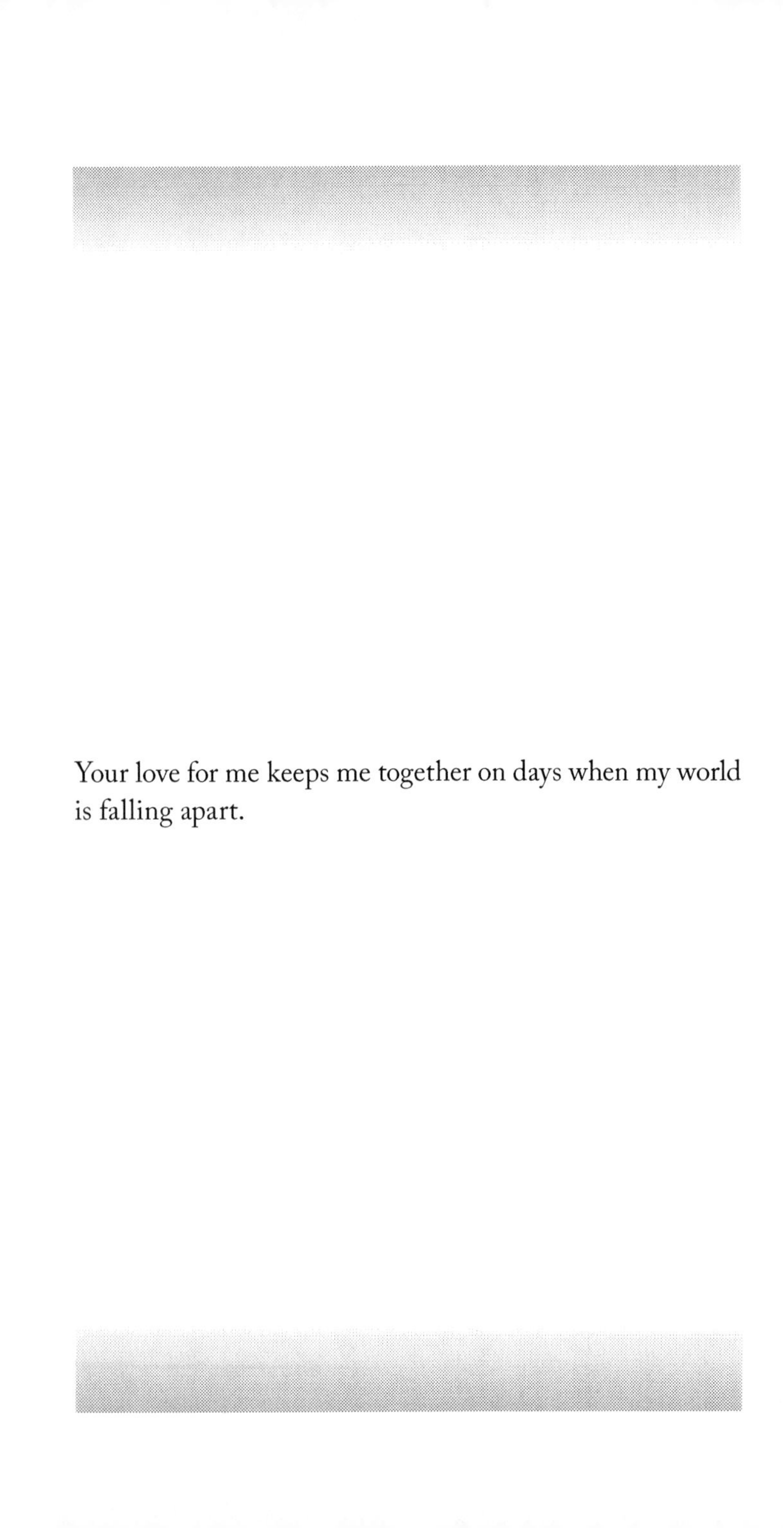

Your love for me keeps me together on days when my world is falling apart.

Chapter 5

Making It Official

Jesus answered, "Most assuredly, I say to you, unless one is born of water and the Spirit, he cannot enter the kingdom of God. That which is born of the flesh is flesh, and that which is born of the Spirit is spirit. Do not marvel that I said to you, 'You must be born again.' The wind blows where it wishes, and you hear the sound of it, but cannot tell where it comes from and where it goes. So is everyone who is born of the Spirit."

—John 3:5–8

I was standing alongside two others with cold shivers running down my spine. The head pastor had asked everyone who was sure they were on their way to heaven sit down, with the rest remaining standing. I'd only remained standing because I hadn't thought that anyone would sit down. I initially thought it was a trick question, only later realising that it was a salvation call. *How can you tell whether you will make it to heaven?* I asked myself. "Can it be possible that all these people are perfect enough to be on their way to heaven?" I mumbled under my breath.

What I didn't realise was that the salvation call is a continuous journey. Looking back now, I can truly say that God intended for it to be that way. He understood my heart and did everything possible to keep me standing on that day in March 2008; left to myself, I would have been overwhelmed by the many glances on that fateful day. The three of us still standing were asked to step forward to the altar. I said the sinner's prayer, and from then onward my spiritual journey began. I truly rededicated my life to Christ and was set on course to start running my race.

> *Whoever seeks to save his life will lose it, and whoever loses his life will preserve it.*
>
> *—Luke 17:33*

> *And I will give you shepherds according to my heart, who will feed you with knowledge and understanding.*
>
> *—Jeremiah 3:15*

I joined the discipleship class, where I learned about the Bible and faith in great detail. I had always read my Bible but mostly Psalms and Ecclesiastes. The other chapters to me were like studying physics or chemistry. I kept at it and engaged in conversations, even when I sometimes felt shy, like when it wasn't my usual circle. I either trembled when joining in or experienced palpitations when I answered a question. The experience felt different. There was something definitely going on, on the inside for sure, that I was unable to explain. Sometimes I was confused; other times I was super excited. I still remember my response to a question asked in the discipleship class about where each one of us was in our spiritual journey: "I am finding myself," I responded. I don't even know how I remember these things.

God began to lead people my way, people who helped me in my new path. One of the teachers from my discipleship class invited me to one of the Light Houses. I remember stepping into this cell group and being overwhelmed by the strange faces. They were either working in the city or doing great stuff that just seemed unattainable to me at the time. I was a little insecure but still managed to engage in conversations and enjoy the great fellowship that day.

It was not a great time in my life, despite just having rededicated my life to Christ. I was a little disturbed by my emotional issues, failed friendships, and my recently ended relationship of five years. Somehow, however, the company of this group was somewhat comforting and refreshing. I had travelled all the way from North London to the other end of South East London for this meeting regardless, so I made the effort, and it was certainly worth it. I met some amazing people and made new friends. During the meeting this particular mister wouldn't stop talking about his twin brother's upcoming nuptials and how he was really excited for him. He even asked everyone to pray along with him for the couple as they approached their big day. I wondered why he was going on and on about it with such vigorous passion. He was one of those who extended a warm welcome to me as a first-timer, grinning from ear-to-ear. I didn't realise at the time that he would one day be my darling husband.

> *The older women likewise, that they be reverent in behaviour, not slanderers, not given to much wine, teachers of good things—that*

> *they admonish the young women to love their husbands, to love their children, to be discreet, chaste, homemakers, good, obedient to their own husbands, that the word of God may not be blasphemed.*
>
> —*Titus 2:3–5*

There was an initiative for young women at Trinity Chapel spearheaded by a phenomenal lady at the time, and based on the book *Kissed the Girls* by Lisa Bevere. I joined one of the cells related to this initiative. The meetings took place very far from where I lived, but I thought it was a good idea to commit to the meetings. The discussions covered topics like purity, identity, relationships, and much more. It was so refreshing, as I had never seen Christians so real in my life before. I had no choice but to open up to some extent at those meetings, because the other women involved were really open too. It was through this initiative that I discovered even more about myself, my journey, our redemption from past mistakes, and the amazing future ahead that is packaged for those who love God and are called by His name.

> *Again I will build you, and you shall be rebuilt, O virgin of Israel! You shall again be adorned with your tambourines, and shall go forth in the dances of those who rejoice.*
>
> —*Jeremiah 31:4*

After one of the sessions I got really emotional, and the facilitator of my cell who is now a darling sister; sent me the above scripture and encouraged me. I was truly encouraged and uplifted as she shared the amazing things she believed God had in mind for me. It was indeed edifying. At another following session, she laid her hands on me and the ladies as we prayed, and I received the Holy Spirit. I couldn't believe it. Strange words began to flow out of my mouth; I was speaking in tongues, something I never imagined I would be doing. I had heard it a few times at churches back home in Ogudu and maybe even in other churches and prayer groups here in England. I'd always found it amusing, but I'd never thought it was something I would do. It was very exciting indeed.

I'm the most gregarious of men and love good company but never less alone when alone.

—Peter O'Toole

But you shall receive power when the Holy Spirit has come upon you; and you shall be witnesses to Me in Jerusalem, and in all Judea and Samaria, and to the end of the earth.

—Acts 1:8

Likewise, the Spirit also helps in our weaknesses. For we do not know what we should pray for as we ought, but the Spirit Himself makes intercession for us with groanings which cannot be uttered.

—Romans 8:26

For he who speaks in a tongue does not speak to men but to God, for no one understands him; however, in the spirit he speaks mysteries.

—1 Corinthians 14:2

My new sister-friend followed up to ensure the experience stayed with me. We prayed together in tongues for at least an hour each week, and soon it became another means to express myself and to communicate my heart to God. What a privilege to be speaking mysteries. My relationship with God started getting real, especially with little answered prayers, like a seat on a packed train, a random act of kindness, and many others like this.

A guest pastor at Trinity Chapel preached a sermon on taking territories. The ushers passed round a tray of nails for us. We were to plant our nails wherever we desired to take territory as an act of faith. I took about three to the front yard of my university in Luton, where I was studying for my master's degree at the time, because I was contemplating facilitating a *Kissed the Girls* group for university students with a friend of mine at her flat in Luton. Of course I was shy about putting the nails in the ground, so I pretended as if I'd dropped something on my way home from lectures one faithful day, and then I quickly put the nails in the ground when no one was looking. It's absolutely hilarious when I remember this now, but I found a way round my shyness.

> *And these signs will follow those who believe: In my name they will cast out demons; they will speak in new tongues; they will take up serpents; with their hands; and if they drink anything deadly, it will by no means hurt them; they will lay hands on the sick, and they will recover.*
>
> —*Mark 16:17–19*

I was so nervous, yet I stepped forward to facilitate a *Kissed the Girls* group. What were the chances that the publicity on my Facebook page and my timid sharing of flyers would bring anyone to the meetings? Just before the sessions were to start, I approached a pregnant girl in the library after class. I had gone round in my mind, contemplating approaching her. Finally, I got the courage to tell her about the meeting. The look on her face seemed to say, "Like yeah, whatever." I didn't think she would turn up, but, lo and behold, she was one of the nine people who came to the first session. Oh boy did she give me a lot of trouble about the description I gave her over the phone to find our meeting place. Thank God I was patient with her. She soon became one of the early major testimonies in my faith walk as I saw God do extraordinary things in her life.

> *Behold, I will bring health and healing to it; I will heal them and reveal to them the*

abundance of peace and truth. And I will cause the captives of Judah and the captives of Israel to return, and will rebuild those places as at the first. I will cleanse them from all their iniquity by which they have sinned against Me, and I will pardon all their iniquities by which they have sinned and by which they have transgressed against Me Then it shall be to me a name of joy, a praise, and an honor before all nations on earth, who shall hear all the good that I do to them; they shall hear all the good that I do to them; they shall fear and tremble for all the goodness and all the prosperity that I provide for it.

—Jeremiah 33:6–9

Facilitating *Kissed the Girls* led me to amazing discoveries about myself. There were no familiar church faces around, so I had the liberty to be me and not feel under pressure.

I soon came to learn more about the young pregnant lady in the library and her story. She broke down at one of the sessions, and only then did we come to learn of her pain and suffering. She had left her family back home and only just recently had lost her dad. Her boyfriend, who had gotten her pregnant, had abandoned her and left her to her faith. She was already making plans to give the baby away to a local church and move on with her life. She was due in only a few weeks when I first met her, but none of her family members even knew she was pregnant. She had asked God to take her life so many times. She'd also asked God to show her He was there, and just a few days later we'd stepped into her life. Even more shocking, when some of the girls and I took more interest and visited her, she hadn't set up a single thing in her room in anticipation of a baby. It was such a sad situation, and we made up our minds to be there for her, seeing her through and helping her get back on her feet.

> *For I have given you an example, that you should do as I have done to you.*
>
> *—John 13:15*

> *No one has seen God at any time. If we love one another, God abides in us, as His love has been perfected in us.*
>
> *—1 John 4:12*

We encouraged her to keep the child and to tell her mum and siblings about all that had happened whilst she was studying and about the baby she was expecting. Of course, at the time it seemed such a scary thing to ask someone to do, especially someone who had just lost her dad a year ago and was dealing with a heartbreak. God was faithful, and we soon watched this lady's story change. We held her hand as she made that phone call to her mum. They both wept over the phone, after some tongue-lashing of course, but it was worth every second, as her mum soon embraced the situation and was willing to stand by her all the way.

I was so amazed at the mercies of God as I travelled back home from Luton to London that night. Could it be that all my trouble had been a set-up just for this one woman who lived in Luton? Had God disrupted my own plans – or, rather, ordered my steps – in such a way that one who was giving up, feeling depressed, losing hope, feeling rejected and abandoned by God, and living with condemnation would now be loved by a bunch of girls following the lead of a girl who was simply experimenting?

We so loved on her. We organised a baby shower, blessing her with gifts for her unborn child, and she was truly grateful. The time soon came for her to have her baby. I couldn't make it, because I was in London at the time, but my friend Ruky was kind enough to stand by her whilst she had the baby. It was a boy, and she named him David Oluwaseun. What an amazing testimony it was for us to see God redeem, rejuvenate, give hope, restore, and redeem a woman who had totally given up on almost everything. Her family supported her, and the little boy soon became their joy, with her mum saying God had brought back her husband in the boy. The young woman soon finished her degree and moved back home with so much hope and zest for life. It was indeed a wonderful testimony.

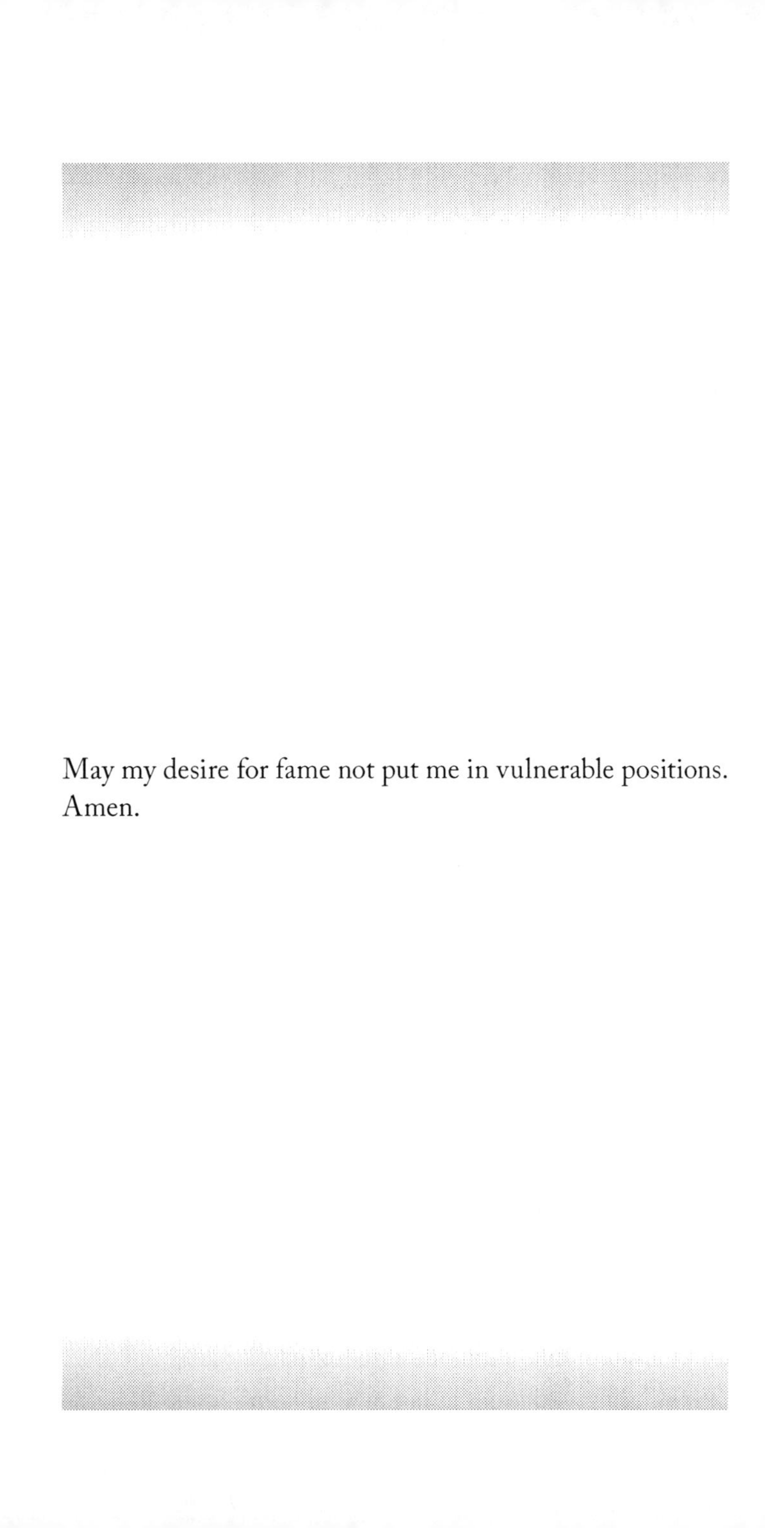

May my desire for fame not put me in vulnerable positions. Amen.

Chapter 6

Service and Finding Boaz

Only fear the Lord, and serve Him in truth with all your heart; for consider what great things He has done for you.

—1 Samuel 12:24

Something spurned me on to serving at my local church, Trinity Chapel. I wanted to do more and be more involved with the happenings at church. After contemplating a department to serve, I decided to volunteer as an usher for one of the midnight services. It was pretty exciting, except that I was sometimes overwhelmed standing in the aisle. I was a little shy, but it was amazing to serve. After the crossover service that year, the amazing members of the ushering team encouraged me to join the department. If I am to be completely honest, I was also persuaded to join because that grinning from ear-to-ear and vigorously passionate brother was also a member of the ushering department. Serving in the ushering department also further helped my spiritual growth; the discipline to arrive early, the dress code, the prayers, and the service were all contributing factors to the strength in my early Christian walk.

> *For you, brethren, have been called to liberty; only do not use liberty as an opportunity for the flesh, but through love serve one another.*
>
> *—Galatians 5:13*

Serving in the ushering department at Trinity Chapel was such an eye-opener to who I was becoming. Not only did it help build my confidence, but it also presented the opportunity to grow alongside diverse personalities and, more importantly, stay accountable to leadership. It was in the middle of this new-found path that God blessed me with the gift of my husband and truly revealed the many areas of my life where I was still suffering major insecurity issues. Although my husband and I are both Nigerian by birth, my husband was born and raised in the United Kingdom, and of course our values naturally differ in some areas of life. Meeting him was certainly a breath of fresh air but was also a challenge to me in many ways. I was fascinated by his refined manner and intrigued by his genuine love for God.

> *Behold I will do a new thing, now it shall spring forth; shall you not know it? I will even make a road in the wilderness and rivers in the desert.*
>
> *—Isaiah 43:19*

It was exciting to sense that this man was interested in me, but I was battling with thoughts about my past, the things I had been used to, and the many ways I had grown to understand relationships. I failed to see what God was doing in my life and just basked in the thought of having a handsome, sought-after boyfriend at the time. God began to expose the areas of my heart that were not right. Oftentimes I felt as if Olawale was showing way too much love; other times I was intimidated by his circle of friendships, when it was obvious that they were very different to me. Olawale was facilitating the house cell group Tawney Road Fellowship at the time. When I look back now, I see this cell group was also a blessing, in the sense that I was challenged to join in conversations and contribute wholly, truly expressing myself unashamedly. It was very difficult for me at the time, as each time I contributed in the fellowship, my heart raced and my voice trembled. All in all, these experiences contributed wholly to my pruning and the becoming of who I am today.

Give me one beautiful holy passion,

Give me one magnificent obsession,

Give me one glorious ambition for my life:

To know and follow hard after You.

Lead me on, and I will run after You.

> *And do not be conformed to this world, but be transformed by the renewing of your mind, that you may prove what is that good and acceptable and perfect will of God.*
>
> —*Romans 12:2*

Gradually, God broke down the walls of my heart, showing me areas where I needed development. It was, as always, a painful process, but it's all been worth it. I soon started embracing my new path, learning to love and give, coming out of myself a bit more, and making efforts with people I would normally not engage with. Simply put, the circumstances pulled me out of my comfort zone, and I truly began to grow.

Olawale was also such a blessing, but you can trust that I gave him a hard time when it seemed to be taking him so long to make the decision about taking things further. It can be all too stressful answering questions about your relationship. I think women are often faced with such pressures, even inside the church. Standing in the middle of my apartment one sunny afternoon, I took out my Bible and asked God to confirm if this was the man He had desired for me, so I could relax in His peace, as I was beginning to get really frustrated at what seemed like slow decision-making on Olawale's part. Lo and behold, I came across this scripture that calmed the waters: "Listen, O daughter, consider and incline your ear; Forget your own people also, and your father's house; so the King will greatly desire your beauty; because He is your Lord, worship Him" (Psalm 45:10–11).

The Word meant so much to me that I soon found my peace and knew for a fact that Olawale would be my husband. When the opportunity presented itself on one of our dates,

I got the courage to ask the all-important question, "Where is this all going?" At first I was overwhelmed with Olawale's embarrassing response: "I am taking my time because I am praying about it." Then I knew God needed me to work on my patience too. Olawale and I soon made our relationship official in the fall of August 2009, and it was the beginning indeed of something new and refreshing. There were so many dots to connect, both our love for God and our flare for writing. Although we still clashed from time to time over issues regarding our values, there was a peace in my heart about God's leading in my life concerning marriage. Even though the relationship may not have ticked all boxes in my eyes, it was one of purpose and certainly more important than my own desires.

> *These things I have spoken to you, that in Me you may have peace. In the world you will have tribulation; but be of good cheer, I have overcome the world.*
>
> —*John 16:33*

In the middle of what seemed like pure bliss was the predicament of my residential status. I had tried to extend my study visa, in the hope that I would stay in London to finish up my master's and then apply for a work permit. However, the home office became a pain in my side, and all my efforts proved futile. After several back-and-forths, indecisions, and court hearings, I'd had enough of the merry-go-round. I came to a firm decision with my family and Olawale, my fiancé at the time, that I would go back to Nigeria to start my time with the National Youth Service Corps (NYSC). It was not the most satisfying decision to be honest, as Olawale and I were just one year into our relationship. Olawale also wasn't pleased with the idea of spending the later part of our courtship distant. You can be sure it was one of the hardest thing to do, especially settling disputes across shores. It had to be done, though, so I packed my bags and made the big move to Nigeria, in the hope that, in time, I would get married, complete the last pending paper for my professional exams (ACCA), and then move back to England on a spousal visa. All these plans I had, and God honoured them indeed.

> *And the Lord said, "Simon, Simon! Indeed, Satan has asked for you, that he may sift you as wheat. But I have prayed for you, that your faith should not fail; and when you have returned to Me, strengthen your brethren."*
>
> *—Luke 22:31–32*

Moving back to Nigeria was definitely something, a different territory altogether. I might have grown up in this great nation, but coming back to it as an adult was quite challenging, especially since most of my adult years had been spent in another country, where I'd formed many values. It was that much more difficult going there as an intentional Christian. It was truly an eye-opener, not just because of the quirks of the country itself but also because of the person I really was on the inside. The move back to Nigeria revealed to me the many areas where I was still lacking in character, and on some occasions I must say it was a very embarrassing sight. The temptations of the flesh faced there were raised to the power of 100: from adhering to traffic laws to staying humble and being the person I was called to be. I would say it was a necessary move, as it helped me discover interesting facts about myself. I developed lots of friendships during my service year, engaging various personalities from different backgrounds and walks of life. I also engaged in social activities and community development that exposed my leadership tendencies.

> *Be of the same mind towards one another. Do not set you mind on high things, but associate with the humble. Do not be wise in your own opinion.*
>
> —*Romans 12:16*

Any Nigerian that is being honest will admit that one of our greatest challenges is the need to be somebody and the need to be associated with or highly regarded by prominent people. A lot of people struggle with being taken for granted, as being appreciated means a lot to them personally. Being taken for granted can be hurtful to them even when those taking them for granted have no intention of undermining who they are. Granted, some ignorant people cause others to stumble in trying to prove themselves above others in one way or the other, but a truly secure mind needn't any approval, affirmation, or control to stay relevant. It was these and many things I learned during my time in Nigeria. Each day God helped me to forge ahead and claim small victories here and there. I soon found in my journey that ordinary people could be one sweet enigma to unravel as you embraced their simple and free outlook on life. There is so much you can learn from ordinary people. Never look down on others.

People are to be loved; God is to be feared. Don't get it twisted!

> *Not forsaking the assembling of ourselves together, as is the manner of some, but exhorting one another, and so much the more as you see the Day approaching.*
>
> —*Hebrews 10:25*

I have always had love for people. I like being around people and talking about all kinds of stuff in this world, especially faith. In addition to God's blessings of the Daystar Christian Centre and the house fellowship. He also blessed my life by surrounding me with amazing women. Soon an idea dropped into my spirit: I should start a ladies fellowship. I took the bold step straight away. I have always been passionate about women, and it was such a blessing to meet with these amazing women from time to time. I guess our meetings also brought about some sanity, letting us know we weren't alone in our struggles. God is kind, and He always blesses us with the love of strangers. We are never left alone in the challenging phases of our lives. We are never alone indeed.

> *No evil shall befall you, nor shall any plague come near your dwelling.*
>
> —*Psalm 91:10*

When I look back now, I give God all the praise for ordering my steps in the year I came home for service. What seemed like a major setback regarding my visa was just God's plan for me to be at home looking after my dad. That year my parents were both ill, with Dad with me in Nigeria and Mum battling for her life in Canada, where she lived with the rest of my younger siblings. Their illnesses really tested my faith. As easy as it is to always attribute bad things like this to spiritual forces somewhere, it's never really been my battle focus. The Word of the Lord does not lie. Even when it seems like there is evil, the Bible is clear on the matter: "So shall they fear the name of the Lord from the west and His glory from the rising of the sun. When the enemy comes in like a flood, the Spirit of the Lord will lift up a standard against him" (Isaiah 59:19).

God stood by His Word, and my parents were whole in no time. There are too many great testimonies to count and many great works at the hands of the Lord; some of them I may not even remember anymore. My year in Nigeria was lovely and gave me the chance to bond with my dad before he later gave my hand in marriage to my husband. One of my fondest memories of my parents is when I finally got the results of the last exam of my ACCA qualifications. I had been under so much stress and was just trusting in God that I had excelled in the last paper. On the day I got my result, I sprinted to my parents' room to tell them the great news (Mum was back from Canada). I will never forget how my dad responded: he picked me all the way up. Even I was shocked, as big a lady as I was, but that didn't stop him. We were filled with so much joy that day. This memory certainly makes up for all the combats we engaged in, in preparation for my wedding. I love you, Mum and Dad.

Dear Lord,

I am so sorry. I'm here again, so hurt. I allow myself to get here. I am really sorry.

You are my joy, and You complete me; no one else does. Help me today to find strength in You.

Chapter 7

We Are Married – Now What?

And said, for this reason a man shall leave his father and mother and be joined to his wife, and the two will become one flesh?
—Matthew 19:5

It could only have been due to God that my spousal visa came in from the embassy just eleven days after my application. Because of the issues surrounding my visa before I left for Nigeria, I had been a little concerned that getting my spousal visa would take a long time. What had once been a real pain suddenly became the easiest thing to get. The visa was all ready for me just after I finished the NYSC programme and was ready to join my husband in England. Before it had seemed like a door was shut, but now everything fell into place with the loving nudge of the one who is meticulous about our lives. With the unfolding events, it was clear that God ordered my steps to Nigeria that year, and when my time was up, He made it all work out. Indeed, God makes all things beautiful in time.

Again the word of the Lord came to me, saying, "As for you, son of man, take a stick for yourself

> *and write on it: 'For Judah and for the children of Israel, his companions.' Then take another stick and write on it, 'For Joseph, the stick of Ephraim, and for all the house of Israel, his companions.' Then join them one to another for yourself into one stick, and they will become one in your hand. And when the children of your people speak to you, saying, 'Will you not show us what you mean by these?'—say to them, 'Thus says the Lord God: "Surely I will take the stick of Joseph, which is in the hand of Ephraim, and the tribes of Israel, his companions; and I will join them with it, with the stick of Judah, and make them one stick, and they will be one in My hand."'"*
>
> —*Ezekiel 37:15–19*

As you would expect of any long-distance relationship, being away from each other during the time I was away in Nigeria was very challenging for Olawale and me. We made it through the hurdles somehow, and I soon moved to England to live with my husband. The first few weeks were exciting. We were house-hunting, visiting places together, and just enjoying the attention we received from family and friends for starting our lives together. We soon began to discover our differences, but God helped us through. As long as we were able to apologise when necessary, we were good. Being newly married was the best feeling ever for me, playing the role of a wife and enjoying the company of my other half.

But as months slowly started to go by, the reality of not getting a job as quick as I'd thought I would hit home. I had all these plans in my heart to find a job, contribute money into the family pot, and be able to buy things round the house, but life just happened. Things didn't quite turn out how I imagined. It was not my ideal for my husband take responsibility for everything; it was not my ideal to have several qualifications and no opportunities to earn a living. I wished getting a job was simple. After all, it was only a job; surely that should have been very easy for God.

> *A man's heart plans his way, But the Lord directs his steps.*
>
> —*Proverbs 16:9*

I received so many rejection letters I lost count of them. Many people told me what I could do better, how many jobs to apply for each day, and what I could be doing whilst I waited for the job to come. The rejections became too many, and I began to lose my self-confidence. I couldn't wrap my head round why no one would even give me a chance. I took on voluntary positions, worked with a friend that knew a friend, worked for the church, and attempted to start a business with some friends, all to no success. How was it that brand-new graduates could bag themselves jobs in the twinkle of an eye whilst I was constantly told I was overqualified or just not right for the position or received no response at all. It began to get really lonely, frustrating, and tiring sitting at home. I sometimes threw temper tantrums at my poor husband, who was trying everything he could to support and encourage me not to give up. When I listened to friends talk about their jobs, organisations, and career paths, I tried to pull a smile each time, but such conversations left me even more devastated, worrying about why my own life had to be any different, why I had to face these delays in my life. It was just a job

I was asking for. Why wouldn't God answer my prayers or the prayers of my pastors, parents, husband, siblings, family members, and friends that cared about my getting a job?

Dear Lord,

Today I have all kinds of emotions spiralling around in my mind. I am not sure where I am with You, but I am familiar with Your Word that You love me no matter what. I hold on to that as my truth. It's not easy to take up one's cross and follow You daily, but hopefully I am learning to be a lot more compassionate, forgiving, patient, loving, and obedient. I trust You are leading my life in the direction You want it to go. It is hard on the flesh, but it will certainly be worth it.

I am grateful for the call upon my life. In order not to take Your mercy for granted, I will need to look inward and deal with my weaknesses so that I may live this life You have called me to live. I have my fears, my reservations, and my fair share of disappointments, but they do not change who You are. I am only going to be a better person. I wish things were easier. I wish life went more smoothly, but challenges can be opportunities for success.

In the midst of my fears and uncertainties I still find Your presence so close, so comforting. You are such a friend, so loving, so forgiving, and so merciful. I don't know how I'll get through, but I know You want to give me something better, and so I'll sacrificially lay down that which I've held on to for so long and walk this journey with You.

You mean the world to me.

> *Hope deferred makes the heart sick, But when the desire comes, it is a tree of life.*
>
> —*Proverbs 13:12*

> *A friend loves at all times, and a brother is born for adversity.*
>
> —*Proverbs 17:17*

Although hope deferred makes the heart sick, God never leaves us alone in our trials. He surrounds us with people who encourage us and help us get by, even strangers. Many people encouraged and helped me, either with personal testimonies, referrals, prayers and check-ups, or spiritual guidance. There was a sister-friend in particular who helped me grow in my spiritual walk in this season from the early-morning 5 a.m. drill (Bible study) to the prayer sessions where we just spoke in tongues for a while.

I began to develop myself more in the Word, listening to sermons when I could and trying to stay as encouraged as I could. Then one day all the little confidence I had been building crumbled. Another friend had told me about an available position as a personal assistant to the office of Sarah Brown, the wife of former prime minister Gordon Brown. By this time, I was happy to take on anything and wasn't fussy about my qualifications. As you can imagine, I was elated by the idea of this position, more so because of who I would be working with. I thought this was definitely God's work. Who knew, perhaps this was His perfect plan to compensate me double for my trouble. It would be an amazing testimony to share with friends and family. I was so short-sighted I failed to see how I had limited God within my mind by my poor thoughts.

I was called in for an interview. I hoped they would be impressed by my qualifications. After all, it was just an administrative/personal assistant role, so why would I be turned down for it in the first place? I was so confident on the day of the interview when I walked into the prestigious building on Liverpool Street. It all seemed so prestigious. I had never been into any buildings like that in my life, and it would definitely be a glamorous building to walk into every morning. I had the interview and was warmly received. I was so certain the job was mine. A few days later, I received a phone call telling me I hadn't gotten the position. Oh, I wept so much and so loudly. I wasn't sure which hurt the most: the fact that I'd been turned down for an administrative position or the fact that I felt as if God had just teased me with a bone. I was really devastated, but God comforted me soon after with His Word, and I began to hope again. I soon began to dream, and I encouraged myself in the Lord.

> *Jesus answered and said to her, "Whoever drinks of this water will thirst again, but whoever drinks of the water that I shall give him will never thirst. But the water that I shall give him will become in him a fountain of water springing up into everlasting life." The woman said to Him, "Sir, give me this water, that I may not thirst, nor come here to draw."*
>
> *—John 4:13–15*

Dear Lord,

Thank You for the many opportunities You have given me in life. Thank You for giving me many second chances that I haven't deserved and for stretching out Your arms to me. I have questions, and there are issues in my life that are still pending. I pray You give me clarity and wisdom and, when the time is truly right, help me to make the moves You really want me to make.

Lord, I just want to please You with every aspect of my life. I want to love You with everything I have. There are too many things that are going on in my heart right now. I am so needy. Lord, fill this void in my heart and help me to totally surrender to You with everything. It's not easy to give up all, take up one's cross, and follow You with everything, but I will get there. This too shall pass. Please heal my heart and help me to love all the things You give me and to be truly content with the relationships I have.

Sometimes it gets tiring, but You are the strength of my life and my portion for evermore. I love You, Lord, maybe not with my whole heart but with my whole mind. I pray today that I get to love You with my whole heart.

I began to bask in the Word of God, studying the scriptures during my lonely hours. God began to teach me His Word. Delighting in the truth of His Word gave me a different perspective to life, brought a new meaning to my life. It wasn't that I didn't desire a job anymore or that I didn't desire any of the other things my contemporaries owned; I just found my peace in God's Word, and somehow my contentment began to grow. I was in my happy place. It may not have appeared that way to everyone who cared about me at that time, but there was a joy that sprung forth from knowing more about Jesus. I was bubbling in revelation, and my confidence and self-esteem began to take on new dimensions. At one point I was even saying to my husband that I didn't think the nine-to-five work life was for me. I found joy in other things that I had. Of course if a job did come, I would be grateful, but I found a way to live and be happy even without the things I once thought I was supposed to have. This new-found peace poured out into my life, even into my marriage – so much so that I began to overlook the things that had been issues in my marriage and in other relationships and learned to submit, love, and forgive. God's strength was made perfect in my weaknesses. Out of this excitement I would share some of my thoughts and revelations on social media, to anyone who cared to listen.

> *Also it is not good for a soul to be without knowledge, and he sins who hastens who hastens with his feet.*
>
> —*Proverbs 19:2*

> *A prudent man conceals knowledge, But the heart of fools proclaims foolishness.*
>
> —*Proverbs 12:23*

When I remember some of my posts, I sometimes cover my face, 'Because I don't believe I was mature enough to handle the delivery of some of the things I shared about the scriptures. As far as I was concerned, I knew what I knew, and I had to fight for the gospel. I still had a lot of growing up to do. However, I shared my faith with so much passion, confidence, and fearlessness. Everything seemed to be going OK until my tragedy struck.

Dearest Father,

My everything, I haven't penned my thoughts in a while. But I'm in this dry place where everything seems cloudy. I am not sure I understand the things You do in my life. Thank You for helping me catch my breath through the nothingness of life. Thank You for the gifts You have given me. Thank You for showing me that I am blessed and marked for greatness even when in reality it seems otherwise. Show me Your manifest presence; help me trust You. Help me stop seeking love in the wrong places. Help me keep my focus on the things that matter the most, which is that You love me and are forever constant in my life.

Help me submit to Your will; help me surrender to Your call over my life. Help me know that even when I don't understand everything, I am still loved and it's OK.

Chapter 8

The Test and the Testimony

But recall the former days in which, after you were illuminated, you endured a great struggle with sufferings: partly while you were made a spectacle both by reproaches and tribulations, and partly while you became companions of those who were so treated; for you had compassion on me in my chains, and joyfully accepted the plundering of your goods, knowing that you have a better and an enduring possession for yourselves in heaven. Therefore do not cast away your confidence, which has great reward. For you have need of endurance, so that after you have done the will of God, you may receive the promise: "For yet a little while, And He who is coming will come and will not tarry. Now the just shall live by faith; But if anyone draws back, my soul has no pleasure in him." But we are not of those who draw back to perdition, but of those who believe to the saving of the soul.

—Hebrews 10:32–39

It was a few hours before the year 2013. My husband and I chose to pass on the usual watchnight service bandwagon. Instead we stayed home, laying all that we desired before God and seeking His face for a promise-word for 2013. Eventually my husband nodded off, leaving me to my own devices, bless him. I was tired that evening myself but was determined to spend some time in God's presence no matter how short. Soon God led me to the above scripture that I don't think I'll ever forget. When I saw it, I leapt for joy, danced around the living room, jumped, and sang praises to Him, particularly for the portion that read, "after you have done the will of God, you may receive the promise." Perhaps my year had finally come, the year the Lord was going to fulfil all His promises to me. I shared the scripture with my husband the following morning. Both of us rejoiced, full of expectations and trusting that it was our year indeed.

Barely two months into the year, I found myself in a strange place in my life, and I was admitted to a mental health clinic, with my husband and other family members visiting me daily. Apparently I had been putting up strange Facebook posts, sending strange messages to friends on my contact list, and basically just doing lots of strange things. Then one day I hadn't shown up at the airport to pick up my father when I was meant to. My dad had called my husband, who was at work at the time, and the two of them had frantically called my phone trying to find me. Finally, my hubby had decided to leave work and headed home, where he had left me that same morning. He'd arrived at home only to find me in bed in a deep sleep. When he'd woken me up, I'd begun to scream – I had lost my mind for real.

I was bombarded with unhelpful comments and questions I had no answers to: "Are you sure you weren't depressed and just didn't know?" "You should have shared what you were going through with us." "Why were you thinking so much?" "Marriage is not easy." "This country can be very lonely." And on and on. I ended up just nodding along in agreement. After all, what was I to do? Some of these questions almost made me raise my fist up at God and ask, "Why? What happened? How did I get here?" A year and a half later, when I was well into my recovery stage, I stumbled on Hebrews 10:32–39 again, and the scripture started to genuinely mean more to me than just mere written promises on the pages of a book.

This period of my life was the most confusing and mysterious time in my life yet: I could not understand it. I could not reconcile why God would not give me the things I desired at the time and then see me rediscover my joy and learn to bask in Him, only to eventually allow such tragedy to befall me. I went through many interpretations in my mind. Maybe it was spiritual? Maybe it was me? In the end, however, none of that really mattered to me. What mattered was that I was in a relationship with God and He had promised to keep me, so why did the reverse seem to be the case?

The doctors referred to my condition at the time as a "psychotic episode". I became dependent on medication, but the medication did not make it any better. The panic and anxiety attacks that followed (both as a symptom of the illness and a side effect of the medication) were the most frustrating thing I have ever endured in my life – not to mention the hallucinations and hearing weird voices. I still cannot understand how my husband coped throughout that time, but I believe the Lord helped us and stood by us, even when it didn't seem so at the time. Upon my discharge from the hospital I still had to be monitored at home. Since my husband had to travel to China for work for a protracted period (about three months), I went to stay with my mum and siblings in Canada so that I could have the support I needed.

Just being around my siblings helped to some extent, but I still put on so much weight, lost my confidence and zest for life, and struggled with my concentration. Those were some of my darkest days, the worst time in my life. I wasn't sure who I was anymore. My mum, dad, siblings, husband, and in-laws were so supportive throughout that entire season of my life. I am so thankful for each and every one of them.

Dear Lord,

I am amazed by You. You are so kind and merciful to me. Thank You for drawing me from many waters. Thank You for the healing You have started in my home. Thank You for every time You've brought deliverance my way. Thank You for everything You have done. May I from this moment continue to bring glory unto Your name. May I continue to please You with everything I have. Thank You for removing the siege and breaking the chains over my life. Indeed, love covers a multitude of sins, and on this day You've shown me who is boss.

I love You.

Though he slay me, yet will I trust Him; Even so, I will defend my own ways before Him.
—Job 13:15

On returning to the UK and being back with my husband, I hoped that I would be able to resume my "normal" life. I tried going back to my regular routine, but I struggled so much. I was still on my medication and suffering those crazy side effects that came with it. My family suggested I get back into the job hunt, to find something to keep busy. Everyone tried all they could to support me, but I was so broken. My mind was so disturbed; I couldn't even keep still. My husband spoke with a few people in the finance department at his place of work about allowing me to come in and get some work experience, which they did. Whilst I was grateful for the opportunity and thought it would help me recover (neither my husband nor I told my employers about the previous illness), it was the hardest thing I had ever had to do. Getting up each morning was so difficult, as I never slept throughout the night without waking up numerous times. I was always so tired, partly as a side effect of the drug Olanzapine I was taking and partly due to my poor sleeping pattern.

There were only two things I found myself comfortable doing: sleeping and feeling miserable about myself. I managed to get back into church activities and somehow got by. I struggled to read my Bible, though, and it was downhill from then onwards. I mean down, down, downhill. I even reached a point where I genuinely found no reason to live any longer. I shared my suicidal thoughts with a few close people a couple of times. I was tired and, frankly speaking, I didn't see how I would ever recover or ever have the peace I'd once enjoyed in my life. Little did I know that I still hadn't hit rock bottom yet.

My husband had to put up with all of this and more, and he did so whilst showing me nothing but unconditional love, in spite of it all. God never left me by myself. Strangers suddenly became friends who saw me through.

> *And even as they did not like to retain God in their knowledge, God gave them over to a debased mind, to do those things which are not fitting.*
>
> —*Romans 1:28*

> *Behold, I have refined you, but not as silver; I have tested you in the furnace of affliction.*
>
> —*Isaiah 48:10*

Dear Lord,

Today I feel so messed up, almost as if I can see through my weaknesses and through myself at how much anger, bitterness, and unforgiveness lies in my heart and mind. Lord, please help me. I don't feel too good today, but I trust like always You will make it all better. You will give me the courage to be everything that You have called me to be.

I don't want to be a hypocrite. Purge my heart, dear Lord. I want to always be in right standing with You all the days of my life. So, Lord, today I am asking You to speak to my heart, quiet every raging storm, and remove everything in my life that does not bring glory to Your name. I don't want to be just a people pleaser. I want to be a God pleaser above all else.

Sanctify me by the truth of Your Word. Help me to die to self and to anything that does not please You or hinders this race that I'm running. Help me, O Lord, to humble myself and to be submissive, honest, truthful, loving, respectful, and kind. Thank You for pointing these things out to me. Thank You for showing me areas of my life that I still need to work on. Give me the right attitude to win over lawlessness. Let today be worth it by letting me spend it with You. I love You, Lord, because even when I'm in my mess, insecurity, and uncertainty, You love me because nothing can separate us from the love of Christ.

Please cover my marriage and my home with the blood of Jesus. Cover my heart and mind with Your blood. Help me to be a good example. Let my life exemplify Christ and all He stands for. I don't want to run this race or live this life just going through the motions. I want to run this race and live it well.

I love my husband with all my heart. He is the best thing that ever happened to me. My marriage is perfect, holy, sanctified, and pure. Whatever the Lord has joined together, let no man put asunder.

Help me, Lord. Amen!

Despite the people God surrounded me with, I started drifting away from God, and my heart became cold and hard towards everything. Although I was still a part of my regular church activities, my heart was far away, and everything that was preached suddenly seemed strange. Running here and there, finding comfort from place to place, I fell into the Enemy's trap and made terrible choices that led me into many troubles. I was so far gone from God that I didn't even realise it until I finally hit rock bottom, the end of myself, not knowing who I was anymore or what I stood for or what I was about. It was from the frying pan and into the fire like they say. I was lost, and I didn't even recognise myself anymore.

I wept many nights. I was weary, and I felt condemned. I felt wrong in many ways, and no one could help me from my fallen pit. However, the Lord showed me great mercy through friends who stood by me at my lowest, never judging but instead supporting and encouraging me to rise again. Most importantly, my husband never gave up on me at my lowest. He always believed the best in me and saw beauty in the ugliness of my state, hope in hopelessness, and strength in weakness. Olawale stood by me, showed me the love of Christ that changed my world, healed my soul, and gave me many reasons to fight to stand. He gave me even more reasons to know for sure that there was a God who cared deeply about me. Then I knew I had married the right man for me. Then I knew that God had chosen my husband for me and that He was with us even in the fire. I also knew that God loved me even in my mess, even in my vulnerability. He turned it all into a blessing.

> *Do not fear, for I have redeemed you; I have summoned you by name; you are mine. When*

> *you go through deep waters, I will be with you; when you go through rivers of difficulty, you will not drown. When you walk through the fire of oppression, you will not be burned up; the flames will not consume you.*
>
> *—Isaiah 43:3*

> *But the Lord your God refused to listen to Balaam. He turned the intended curse into a blessing because the Lord your God loves you.*
>
> *—Deuteronomy 23:5*

It was in this way that God began to work on my heart. The healing process was not easy, and I cannot remember how the strength came about. As they say, when you are at your very lowest, there is nowhere else to go except up.

In November 2014 I told my doctor I didn't want to continue taking the drugs anymore. He looked at me and said, "At least take them for another six months. People don't just go off drugs like that. You will risk having a relapse." I was fed up of taking the drugs and having to keep going in for seasonal check-ups in the mental health clinic. I didn't want to step foot there any longer. Whilst I sympathised with the patients I'd left behind in that place after I'd been discharged, some far less fortunate than me, I just wanted to be free. I refused to go on another six-month plan, and that was the last day I stepped foot into the hospital for anything mental health related. I have never looked back since then.

My healer, my redeemer, my rescuer,

Right by my side, always.

I have heard of You by the hearing of the year,
but now my eye sees You.

—Job 42:5

There were lots of other areas of my life that God still had to visit, but healing had begun, and it continued until the tragedy that had struck in February 2013 became a distant memory. God had perfected all that had concerned me. My hope began to rise again, and my trust began to blossom. I could see a glimpse of my bright future once more. It wasn't so dark anymore, even though there were many questions still left unanswered in my mind, like, why would You allow this to happen to me? How did I get here? What could I have done wrong for this to happen to me? I may never get answers to these questions whilst I still live here on earth, but I know these two things: I now have a story to share that will bless someone, and all things work together for the good of those who love God and are called according to His purpose.

And we know that all things work together for good to those who love God, to those who are called according to His purpose.

—Romans 8:28

In the meantime, I joined a project management course with the company Almond Careers in the hope that it would help me get back on track. It was really refreshing. I regained my confidence, joined in with the activities, and even made a few new friends. I realised before long that I now had the confidence to go back on the job hunt.

A close friend of mine had been hired by a company in Nigeria in 2012, just at the time she was getting married and shortly after we had both finished our service in the NYSC. When she'd told me back then that she had flown to the UK for her interview as a step of faith and had been given an offer to start soon, I'd thought, *Dear Lord, when will it be my turn? Everyone keeps getting jobs, and I keep roaming aimlessly.* Sometime in late 2013, she encouraged me, as usual, about my jobless situation and said that she was going to speak to her boss to see if I could come on board, even if only to gain some work experience. I was excited at the prospect, but it ended up amounting to little. All my communication with her company quickly went quiet, and I learned they had recruited someone else. I continued in my misery until a glorious, life-changing day in September 2014, when my friend called me to say that her boss had randomly asked about the friend that she'd talked about a while back.

> *When the LORD brought back the captivity of Zion, we were like those who dream. Then our mouth was filled with laughter, and our tongue with singing. Then they said among the nations, "The Lord has done great things for them." The Lord has done great things for us, and we are glad.*
>
> —*Psalm 126:1–3*

It was like a dream. I was called in for a chat and then another interview and then a meeting with HR. I was given a three-month contract with continuous extension until eventually I was awarded a permanent position with a competitive salary package. It took me a while to adjust to the monthly income, but through all of this God showed me that nothing was impossible for Him. He showed me that I didn't need to be strong for Him to do great things in my life. I still pinch myself from time to time in the office, still amazed at how God turned my story around. I remember some of the many things I said to myself or to my husband in my time of despair: "I don't think a job is for me." "I don't think I can ever work in my life." "If God does this one thing for me, I'll know for sure there is nothing He can't do." These thoughts of mine show you how low I thought of myself and how unbelieving my circumstances had made me. God does not lie; He keeps every word of His promises.

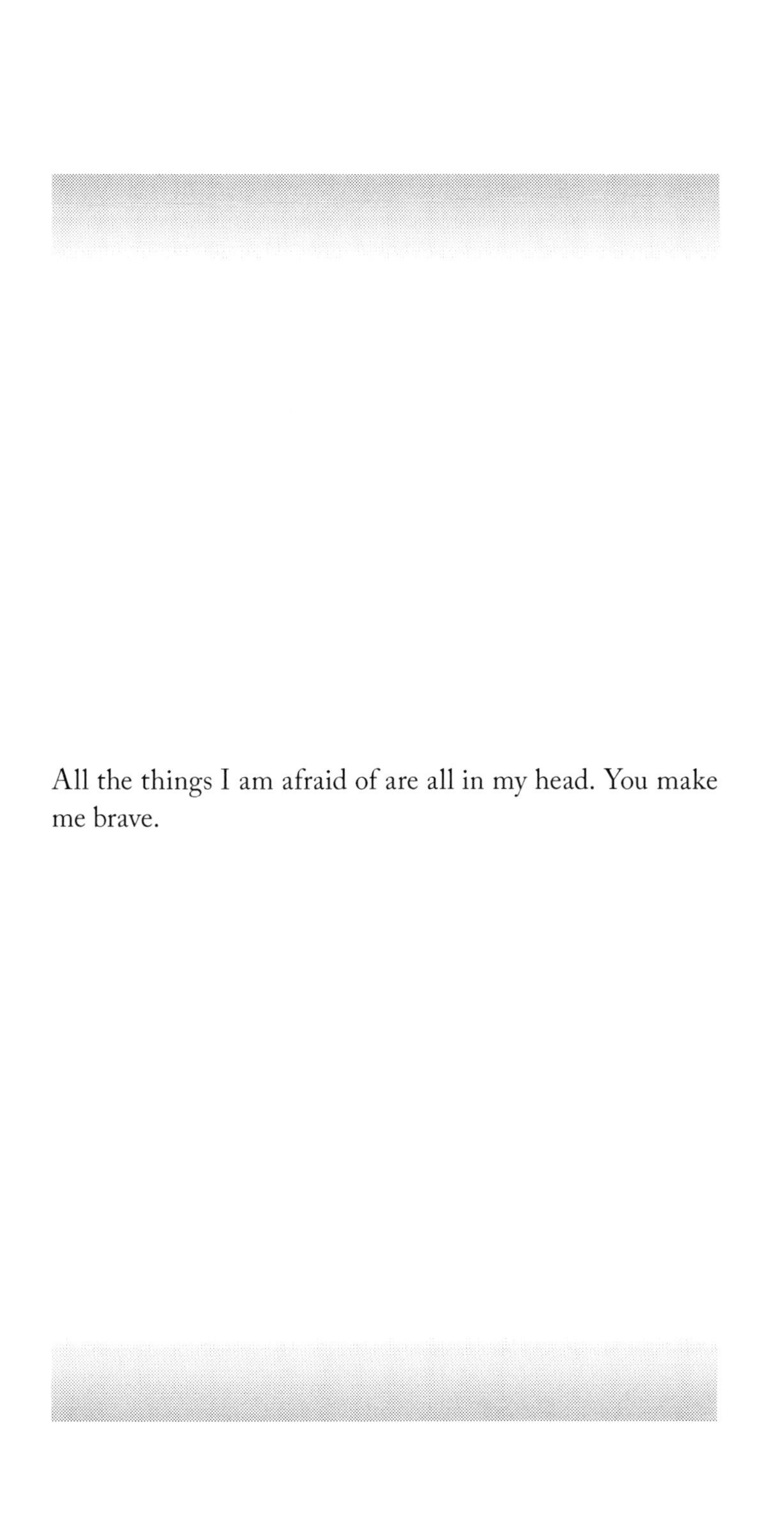

All the things I am afraid of are all in my head. You make me brave.

Chapter 9

My Relationships, My Passion

A man who has friends must himself be friendly, but there is a friend who sticks closer than a brother.

—Proverbs 18:24

I soon discovered in life that your relationships are a big part of searching out who you are, what your passions are, and most of all what your purpose is. Some relationships nurture you, and others test you, but they all help you grow and teach you life lessons one way or the other. I am extroverted by nature and seem to have many people in my life, but only a few people are allowed in my innermost space. Some may argue that I can be extra sensitive, and others may even say that I am complex, but I have grown to see that most of these supposed quirks are a part of who I am, a major reason why I love what I do, and an integral part of what I am called to do in life. I am still learning and discovering myself, but I believe that every relationship must be respected. I also believe that you must do unto others what you would have them do unto you and that you should never say no when it is within your means to help others.

> *Be of the same mind toward one another. Do not set your mind on high things, but associate with the humble. Do not be wise in your own opinion.*
>
> —*Romans 12:16*

There may still be other areas of my life where I need more humility. If there is anything I don't want to ever be in my life, it's proud. I've realised over the course of my growing years that I am drawn towards people of lowly positions. I tend to have a lot of compassion for people who can't fight for themselves, who are treated unfairly, or who are suffering in any way in this already difficult life. I gravitate toward and get along better with these kinds of people, as my gifts thrive better with them.

I have discovered a lot about myself as I have grown older. Previously I thought I struggled to maintain relationships with those who have it all together because of an insecurity issue, but I've come to understand my relationships are all about where I'm going in life. I am passionate about people and feel sheer joy when someone smiles from the heart because of me or when someone is lost for words because I helped them in some way. Who wouldn't feel wonderfully fulfilled by that?

> *But love your enemies, do good, and lend, hoping for nothing in return; and your reward will be great, and you will be sons of the Most High. For He is kind to the unthankful and evil.*
>
> —*Luke 6:35*

Two of the hardest things to do are to love those who don't love you and to forgive those who have hurt you deeply. It is nearly impossible for people who have large hearts in a world where that is scarcely the case to avoid getting hurt. This one thing is true, however: God never forgets all our pains, sufferings, and perseverance. All of these things also build character and tenacity in us so we can function in our God-given purpose, whatever it is we have been created to do. At the time, suffering is always difficult, but I have come to realise that it is always worth it. Out of the rubbles, heartaches, and disappointments is birthed the greatness that is required for our assignment. We should never stay down too long nursing our wounds. We must learn to get up and say to ourselves, "I am growing." At least this has been my motto, and it has always worked in my life.

Dear Lord,

Thank You for today. I really appreciate all that You are doing in my life. I know You are working in my heart. Help me like Hannah to pour out my heart to You, my hurts and my pain. I give my past to You. I give my life to You. Help me to heal. You are dealing with my baggage, and I appreciate You for that. Give me wisdom and insight; help me to be open to Your correction. I don't have much to say. I love You, and I'm sorry for all the idols in my life.

It is well. Amen.

> *Seize life! Eat bread with gusto, Drink wine with a robust heart. Oh yes – God takes pleasure in your pleasure! Dress festively every morning. Don't skimp on colors and scarves. Relish life with the spouse you love. Each and every day of your precarious life. Each day is God's gift. It's all you get in exchange for the hard work of staying alive. Make the most of each one! Whatever turns up, grab it and do it. And heartily! This is your last and only chance at it, For there's neither work to do nor thoughts to think In the company of the dead, where you are most certainly headed.*
>
> *—Ecclesiastes 9:10 (MSG)*

One of the things I struggled with in my earlier days of faith is the misconception that you have to be this sad and grumpy individual glossing over life, dragging your feet as if you were called to live a miserable life. Rather, God derives pleasure from our pleasure, and He created us each uniquely to express who we are and who He has called us to be. Christianity makes us sensible, Christianity makes us selfless, Christianity makes us accommodating, and Christianity allows us to do all things – in moderation, yes, but certainly not dull of expression. The more I pressed in on my relationship with God, the more amazing things I discovered about myself. I realised that God wanted me to express my individuality, albeit in moderation, as much as I myself wanted to do so. God rejoices in our pleasure; you can take that to the bank any day. He is that meticulous.

For you, brethren, have been called to liberty; only do not use liberty as an opportunity for the flesh, but through love serve one another.

—*Galatians 5:13*

Of course we are not called to disrupt others whilst we try to live out our lives, to hurt people in our quest to express who we are, or to disobey God because we are being ourselves. Although we are called to freedom, we are also called to serving each other in love, and our motives and actions shouldn't always be self-seeking. True freedom is the ability to exercise self-control, to deny yourself even when your entire body is screaming self. Only then can you truly say that you are not a slave to anything.

Pure and undefiled religion before God and the Father is this; to visit orphans and widows in their trouble, and to keep oneself unspotted from the world.

—*James 1:27*

God has put good in every single one of us, and we all have a desire to be relevant and to make an impact, either negatively or positively. Deep down inside, we all know that to preserve the longevity of our existence we must mean something to somebody somewhere or do something significant in our world, either as a parent, child, sister, brother, employee, student, or a random writer somewhere. However, there is a force behind every motive, action, and reason. If God is our reason, then the desire to help others, make positive changes, and do something worthwhile is even more evident.

Some days I am so restless. Everything feels kind of dry. I realise how empty the world can be. The world can feel so boring and unexciting during certain seasons. I want to be on the run, moving for God and doing mighty things. I am so bored and uninterested. I can't seem to find anyone who agrees with my thought pattern. I have to be a lot more patient with others.

A PECULIAR FRIEND

> *As each one has received a gift, minister it to one another, as good stewards of the manifold grace of God.*
>
> *—1 Peter 4:10*

Sometimes the things we pray away are the very things God wants to use in our lives to serve a purpose in the lives of others. A knife can be used for many things, including hurting others, but you won't suddenly wake up one morning, grab it from your kitchen top, and go kill someone – I mean for those of us who are normal, that is. For example, I used to complain that I talked way too much, and some of my friends and colleagues confirmed this when I owned up to it. However, after several attempts at trying to be someone I wasn't, I suddenly realised my chattiness was an ability I had been graced with. I just had to learn how to use it well and channel it towards the right cause and in the right direction. A few years ago as I looked back at my life at the many things I'd started and abandoned, I realised that my heart had always called me towards sharing my thoughts, expressing myself outwardly, writing, and participating in any kind of philanthropy through any channel. God uses our experiences as tools to bless others, and the onus is on us to find those things that won't go away, learn how to use them well, and bless the world with what we have been given. I am thankful for my current gifts and for those still yet undiscovered.

Dear Lord,

I am so grateful for You, Lord, for all You are teaching me. I have learned a lot from You this year. I've learned a lot about myself, people, my weaknesses, and my strengths. Thank You for being the Lord of my life. Help me to always be an example of truth. Let my light shine so that all may see Your glory. I'm sorry for not listening to You most of the time, as I always make a mess of everything

Help me to always watch my tongue and my attitude. Help me to always think about You. Help me to have a close relationship with You, so close and dear to You. Thank You for teaching me lessons in this season and preparing me for my family and my ministry.

I love You so much, Lord.

Chapter 10

Jesus Can Be Your Friend Too

For God so loved the world that He gave His only begotten Son, that whoever believes in Him should not perish, but have everlasting life. For God did not send His Son into the world to condemn the world, but that the world through Him might be saved.

—*John 3:16–17*

Despite popular belief, God is not some taskmaster who delights in seeing people go through hell because of their many offences or some foreign authority who is looking forward to hosting thousands in the lake of fire. He is the most compassionate, loving, merciful, and gracious father I know. I have seen it in my life, and although I have not been permitted to fully share my experiences about His mercy, I can vouch for this one truth any day, anytime: God loves you and me, and He does not desire that any of us should perish. In a world that's already full of critics, broken people, judgemental people, and various personalities, it's difficult to see how God loves us, but He certainly does.

The Lord is gracious and full of compassionate, slow to anger and great in mercy.

—Psalm 145:8

The Lord is not slack concerning his promise, as some count slackness; but is longsuffering toward us, not willing that any should perish, but that all should come to repentance.

—2 Peter 3:9

God is long-suffering towards us, His beloved, and His desire is to draw near to us so that He can love us and give us the life He has called us to live. This world can be toxic and challenging to live in most of the time, but we don't have to go through it on our own. You may ask, "But if God is all-powerful, why does He allow all these difficult things to happen in our world?" It was not so from the beginning. God created a perfect world until the Devil, who was once an angel, rebelled against Him and began turning the very world God had created against Him. Why didn't God destroy the Devil immediately, and why has God left him to his vices? It's the concept of free will, which is an idea I believe we have all heard a million times. Although God takes time to execute judgement, He always has a perfect reason for it, and you can be sure that God is always right. He may seem slack concerning His promises or seem slow to react, but He is never out of control. God desires that our decision to love Him is of our own free will. The evils the Enemy uses to oppress us are the very things God uses to build us up. At the end of the day, we always win, and the Enemy always loses; in fact he has already lost.

I've grown to realise absolutely nothing in this world can ever satisfy me. We are all broken, fallible people with different flaws, no matter how put together we seem, and to rely on such security would be foolishness. The only identity that is sure is that of Christ, the begotten Son who was given.

To be loved is magical. To accept love is everything.

And you He made alive, who were dead in trespasses and sins, in which you once walked according to the course of this world, according to the prince of the power of the air, the spirit who now works in the sons of disobedience, among whom also we all once conducted ourselves in the lusts of our flesh, fulfilling the desires of the flesh and of the mind, and were by nature children of wrath, just as the others. But God, who is rich in mercy, because of His great love with which He loved us, even when we were dead in trespasses, made us alive together with Christ (by grace you have been saved).

—Ephesians 2:1–5

Whose unbelieving minds the god of his world hath blinded, lest the light of the glorious Gospel of Christ, who is the image of God, should shine unto them.

—2 Corinthians 4:4

For we are His workmanship, created in Christ Jesus unto good works, which God hath beforehand ordained, that we should walk in them.

—Ephesians 2:10

As cliché as this sounds, God has many great plans for you and me. He decided them long ago, and the only way to be the best you can be is by realising your goals and dreams through Him. You may do all that you can in the flesh, and it may seem like you are achieving worldly success because of validation, popularity, or acquisition of worldly possession; however, true joy can only be derived from a healthy relationship with Christ. This is not to say that we will not face difficulties or stumble whilst we sail through life, but the inner peace and security that comes with the salvation of our soul makes life truly worth living. People will fail us, society will face us, the government will fail us, and even parents and loved ones will sometimes fail us. God is the only constant in life that is guaranteed to be with us through every season. He is that friend you can talk to anytime. He is one who will always comfort you through your struggles; one who is willing to go down with you and up with you, up to the mountains and through the valleys; one who sees your heart and loves you all the same.

> *Jesus answered and said unto her, "Whosoever drinketh of this water shall thirst again, but whosoever drinketh of the water that I shall give him shall never thirst; but the water that I shall give him shall be in him a well of water springing up into everlasting life."*
>
> —*John 4:13–14*

> *When Jesus heard it, He said unto them, "They that are whole have no need of the physician, but they that are sick. I came not to call the righteous, but sinners to repentance." Healthy people don't need a doctor, but the sick. I have not come to call the righteous, but sinners to repentance.*
>
> —*Mark 2:17*

There are many self-righteous Christians in the world today, and it's because they honestly don't know any better. I was once there before until I fell flat on my face and realised I wasn't all that in the first place. There's nothing anyone can do about this truth: love conquers all. We all sin. The fact that some sins carry more consequences than others does not make other sins justified. We are all broken and fallible, and that's why we need Jesus in the first place. He carried all our sins, and because of His sacrifice we no longer need to suffer judgement for all the terrible things we do. Regardless of who you are, where you have been, or how broken or messed up your life may be, God can fix you. The fix is not always instantaneous, but it's always revolutionary. God always leaves us better than He met us; in fact He never leaves us. Don't let others scare you away from the faith and make you think that it's a standard too high to meet. That's their version of who God is. No one is justified by works; we are justified because of the mercies and grace of God.

We do not aspire to remain slaves to sin forever, as God desires for us to be transformed and renewed from the day we come to the faith, becoming better people as we move through life and bringing others into the faith also. But we must first come as we are, empty, honest, and broken before God.

All my life, I always wanted to be somebody. Now I see that I should have been more specific.

—Jane Wagner

But God forbid that I should glory, save in the cross of our Lord Jesus Christ, by whom the world is crucified unto me, and I unto the world.

—Galatians 6:14

And the world passeth away and the lust thereof, but he that doeth the will of God abideth forever.

—1 John 2:17

Jesus said unto her, "I am the resurrection and the life. He that believeth in me, though he were dead, yet shall he live."

—John 11:25

I don't know where you may be in your life, what season you are in at this moment. You may be having good days, bad ones, or even terrifying ones, but I trust God that you are encouraged by my testimony. If you've already surrendered your life to Him, I hope that my account will make you reflect on your own journey so far and continue on the straight and narrow path. If you haven't surrendered your life to Him, if you're still unsure, taking your time, not sure how it all makes sense, I encourage you to accept this friend into your life as your personal Lord and Saviour. It may not be a magical experience, and you may not get all that you want in one day, but I guarantee you that it's one adventurous journey that is sure to lead you to a great destination.

The world is indeed fading away. There are too many dark days currently and still ahead of us, but only those who put their trust in the Lord, who make God their refuge and hiding place, are truly secure. A relationship with Christ gives you a phenomenal identity that helps you to keep your head above water even when it seems like you are drowning. In God there is a confidence that no person or earthly achievement can provide. Most importantly God wants to be a friend to you. He wants to be a part of your everyday life, and He wants to be part of your important moment. You have been through so much; perhaps you've wondered why God allowed you to go through certain things in your life. He can fix your hurts and heal your heart like He healed mine. God longs to hear your voice in the morning, during the day, and at any random time in your life. You don't have to be religious or rigid about how you relate with Him. God desires for you to seek Him out yourself and discover depths of yourself in Him. God loves you, and that's the gospel truth.

> *And you will seek Me and find Me, when you search for me with all your heart.*
>
> *—Jeremiah 29:13*

> *Call to me, and I will answer you, and show you great and mighty things, which you do not know.*
>
> *—Jeremiah 33:3*

> *But as it is written: "Eye has not seen, nor ear heard, nor have entered into the heart of man the things which God has prepared for those who love Him."*
>
> *—1 Corinthians 2:9*

> *My flesh and my heart fail, but God is the strength of my heart and my portion forever.*
>
> *—Psalm 73:26*

For you formed my inward parts; you covered me in my mother's womb. I will praise you, for I am fearfully and wonderfully made; marvellous are your works, and that my soul knows very well. My frame was not hidden from You, when I was made in secret, and skilfully wrought in the lowest parts of the earth. Your eyes saw my substance, being yet unformed. And in Your book they all were written, the days fashioned for me, when as yet there were none of them. How precious also are your thoughts to me, O God! How great is the sum of them.

—Psalm 139:13–14

God loves me, and He certainly loves you too. And it has nothing to do with what you have done, what you are doing, or what you will do in the future. He loves you just because.

About the Book

The book is about the author's personal life journey so far, documenting her rise from challenging and difficult circumstances and sharing how she was able to recover from them. She seeks to encourage, inspire, and edify her readers in the hope that they soon find a new sense and reality.

Printed in the United States
By Bookmasters